WHEAT, WINE & OIL

ELEMENTS OF THE TRUE ANOINTING AND ITS OVERFLOW

OTHER BOOKS BY DR. JOSEPH N. WILLIAMS

The God We Worship

A Conversation with Wisdom

A Conversation with Wisdom (Companion Workbook)

WHEAT, WINE & OIL

Elements of the True Anointing and Its Overflow

with Companion Study Guide

Wheat, Wine & Oil: Elements of the True Anointing & Its Overflow
Copyright © 2015 by Dr. Joseph N. Williams
Printed in the United States of America

ISBN: 978-0-9864305-8-9

All rights reserved. No part of this book may be reproduced or transmitted in any form or by any means, electronic or mechanical, including photocopying and recording, or by any information storage and retrieval system, without permission in writing from the publisher. For permission requests, contact the publisher at the address indicated below.

All Scripture quotations, unless otherwise indicated, are taken from the Holy Bible, King James Version.

Scripture quotations taken from the Amplified® Bible,
Copyright © 1954, 1958, 1962, 1964, 1965, 1987
by The Lockman Foundation.
Used by permission. (www.Lockman.org)

Scripture quotations taken from the New American Standard Bible®, Copyright © 1960, 1962, 1963, 1968, 1971, 1972, 1973,
1975, 1977, 1995 by The Lockman Foundation.
Used by permission. (www.Lockman.org)

"The Bitter Truth" (Revised and adapted for publication.)
Copyright © 2012 by LaSonya Thomas
Used by permission.

Book Cover Design & Layout by Ebony Murdoch

Take thou also unto thee principal spices…And thou shalt make it an oil of holy ointment, an ointment compound after the art of the apothecary: it shall be an holy anointing oil.

…Take unto thee sweet spices…And thou shalt make it a perfume, a confection after the art of the apothecary, tempered together, pure and holy:

Exodus 30:23-25, 34-35

For the LORD hath redeemed Jacob, and ransomed him from the hand of him that was stronger than he. Therefore they shall come and sing in the height of Zion, and shall flow together to the goodness of the LORD, for wheat, and for wine, and for oil, and for the young of the flock and of the herd: and their soul shall be as a watered garden; and they shall not sorrow any more at all.

Jeremiah 31:11-12

Contents

Acknowledgments

Preface … 11

Chapter 1 - The Altar & The Incense … 17

Chapter 2 - Prayer and Intercession … 35

Chapter 3 - From Blessing to Presence … 51

Chapter 4 - Kingdom Connectors … 67

Chapter 5 - The Wheat … 81

Chapter 6 - The Wine … 93

Chapter 7 - The Oil … 107

Study Guide … 129

Notes

Bibliography

VIII

Wheat, Wine & Oil

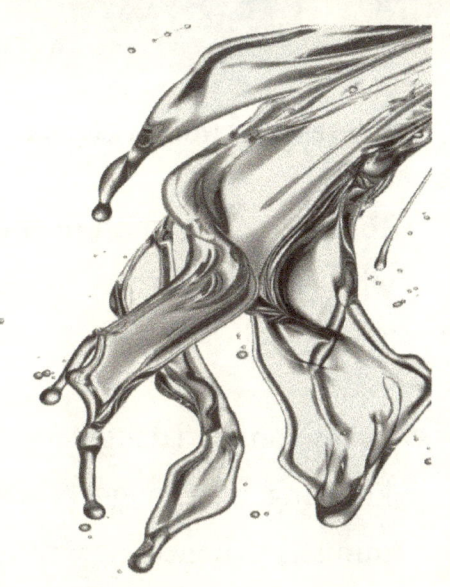

Acknowledgments

I *first give praise to God— in whom I live and move and have my being. I am grateful for another privilege of sharing His Word. The gifts of God demonstrate His goodness to us and gives one the honor of representing Him in various ways to impart, strengthen, encourage, and support others. I humbly acknowledge the following persons:*

To those faithful intercessors who spent their time and resources impacting my life during the early years of my spiritual development with words and deeds of encouragement…that are now a part of the "great cloud of witnesses" awaiting the trumpet call of God to the resurrection of eternal life.

To Carolyn, my faithful and loving wife of 42 years at this writing, who supports the ministry unselfishly with love, prayer and patience. Thank you!

To my sons and daughters of the Christ Church family, who without knowing, gave "nuggets of wisdom" that inspired me through their ministries; hence the writing of this book. I make special mention of the following elders: LaSonya Thomas for her contribution on "The Bitter Truth"; Keiron Phillips, whose anointed protocol and administrative skill has made the Art of the Apothecary services successful time and time again; Adrienne Neal for her clerical support in preparing sermon outlines and lesson plans—often at the last minute; Nicholas Adams and the production team for excellence in preparing screen presentations; and teamwork by the ministry of helps. Thank you!

To Mrs. Ebony Murdoch for your commitment and excellence in editing skills, taking extra time and resources to ensure this project was completed in a timely manner. Thank you!

Preface

More than ever, authentic Christianity in this day and time needs an influx of something greater than mere mental assent and emotion. A true relationship with God cannot flourish without the firm and solid foundation of biblical truth upon which to organize, build, and sustain godly character.

After much thought, prayer, and prodding by the Holy Spirit, I believe this is the right time to offer strength and encouragement to the body of Jesus Christ everywhere. The teachings within these chapters were birthed out of over thirty years of ministry to the community of faithful men, women, and youth known as Christ

Church International in the southeast part of Jamaica, New York.

I follow with honor the precept and example of my late parents, Bishop John C. Williams and Dr. Kathryn J. Williams, who instilled their love for the Word in me from my earliest remembrance. I learned at a young age that it's not what I eat that strengthens me, but what I digest.

> This book is designed to bring you to a deeper experienced reality in your walk with God.

Jesus explained that the present form of the kingdom of God is spiritual and invisible—one must experience new birth in order to see or enter it (John 3:3-5). As the sphere of God's rule, it includes His eternal purpose and all of His works from beginning to end (Acts 15:18; Eph. 3:11). It expands through the world gradually as yeast working through a batch of dough (Matt. 13:33).

The apostle Paul declared that this spiritual kingdom is marked by righteousness, peace, and joy in the Spirit (Luke 17:20; Rom. 14:17). This book is designed to bring you to a deeper experienced reality in your walk with God by teaching you how to walk out these and other kingdom principles.

The Bible speaks of the present state of the church. There are many false teachers who operate through seducing spirits and doctrines of the devil (1 Tim. 4:1-2). There remain those who desire blessings without repentance. Further, they are unable to endure sound doctrine (2 Tim. 4:3). They only desire to have their consciences pacified through slick catch phrases and explore the intricate details of their own thoughts—absent of conviction or revelation. In spite of these and other issues, the anointing yet dwells among true Spirit-filled believers in these end times.

> Be glad then, ye children of Zion, and rejoice in the LORD your God: for he hath given you the former rain moderately, and he will cause to come down for you the rain, the former rain, and the latter rain in the first month. And the floors shall be full of wheat, and the fats shall overflow with wine and oil.
>
> JOEL 2:23-24

The Old Testament speaks prophetically of the day when the Holy Spirit will be poured out afresh on all people, filling them with wheat, wine, and oil— elements that represent an understanding of the Word of God, cleansing by the blood of Jesus Christ, and the anointing of the Holy Spirit.

Each item of the harvest is directly linked to the level of anointing that will be poured out on believers who work the field of the world for Christ. These levels (or stages) are revelation, preparation, and destination. In the first stage, the Holy Spirit gives us illumination out of revelation through inspiration. Revelation in this sense is truth that has been given, uncovered, or unveiled to us. This is not discovered by natural reasoning. It comes from God to man through man. The second stage, preparation, refers to "the process," or the experiences gained by enduring necessary and sufficient testing. Destination, the third stage, refers to where you are spiritually (now) and is connected to where you will be (in the future). Sincere believers often begin to realize they are already walking in their destiny, and with growth and maturation, will accomplish even more for God's kingdom and glory!

In addition to the wheat, wine, and oil, this book also considers the Mosaic Tabernacle as it relates to the oil and incense of God. These studies have far-reaching implications for any who would identify and experience the genuine anointing of the Holy Spirit and the overflow of His presence and power daily.

The material presented here is the fruit of extensive personal study and hermeneutic preparation. My prayer is that this book will be a great blessing to your life, as you seek to mature in the things of God and advance the kingdom in your sphere of life. As you read, take time to look up the scripture references and meditate on them—there is great wealth to be discovered as you do.

Remember, "It is the glory of God to conceal a thing: but the honour of kings is to search out a matter" (Prov. 25:2). To help further this endeavor, a brief study guide has been included at the back of this book.

Dr. Joseph N. Williams
September 30, 2015

High priest offering incense on the altar, as in Leviticus 16:12. Illustration from Henry Davenport Northrop, "Treasures of the Bible," published 1894.

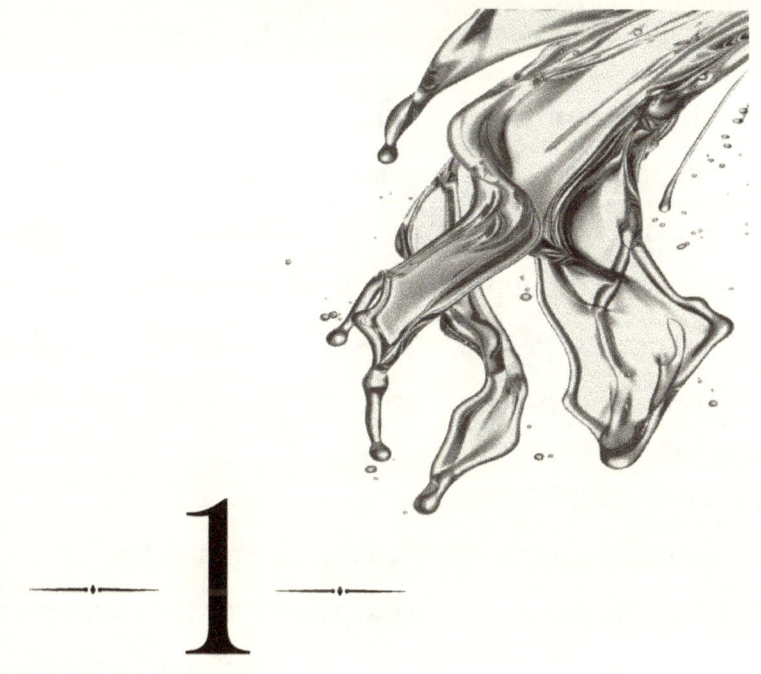

1

The Altar & the Incense

Before we begin to examine elements of the anointing oil and sacred incense, we must draw attention to the fact that in the Old Testament, God intended to have His people conduct worship in a clearly specified manner. This is evidenced by the tabernacle plans given to Moses in the wilderness. We need to understand how these types and truths affect us in this day and time.

Worship in the Wilderness

The account of the construction of the Tabernacle can be found in the book of Exodus, which illuminates three key subjects: Israel's redemption from bondage, the giving of the Law, and the pattern for true worship. Interesting—the Law was given on one hand, and a system of approaching God through sacrifice on the other! The Tabernacle of Moses gives us typical and prophetical symbolism that foreshadows Jesus Christ and His body, the Church.

God gave Moses a detailed blueprint for the construction of a portable sanctuary called the Tabernacle (or Tent of Meeting). Moses then relays the plan to the people, for their support and participation. What was the purpose of this structure? God desired a place—"that I may dwell among them" (Ex. 25:8).

After centuries in bondage, they had no set place to worship the God of their fathers. In Egypt, they were forced to build cities, and may have even helped build temples there (Ex. 1:11). I imagine they were inspired and awed at the prospect of having their own "worship center" in the wilderness.

The Tabernacle had three parts: the Outer Court, the Holy Place, and the Holy of Holies. In the courtyard was the Altar of Burnt Offering and the Brazen Laver. In the Holy Place were the Altar of Incense, Table of Showbread, and Golden Lampstand. Finally, in the Holy of Holies, separated by a high curtain, was the Ark of the Covenant—and the glory of the Lord! (This book only focuses on the Altar of Incense, but the reader is encouraged to study this topic, found in Exodus 31-40, for rich spiritual reward.)

The express purpose for erecting this structure was that Jehovah, the covenant God, might dwell or *abide* among His redeemed people. This also became important because His name would be recorded there. This was the signet of His person and presence among His people.

> This all pointed to the New Testament dwelling place of God. The presence and name of God is to be found "in Christ."

This all pointed to the New Testament dwelling place of God. The presence and name of God is to be found "in Christ." It should be noted that God was very particular about how and where His presence and name would be placed. That principle remains true today. The apostle Paul declared that the body of Christ is "…the fullness of Him that filleth all in all" (Eph. 1:23). The material structures of the Old Testament all bring us to a powerful revelation of the dwelling place of God through the Holy Spirit (Eph. 2:22). Hallelujah!

It is noteworthy that the Tabernacle building project was a team effort. Everyone contributed their time, talents, and resources. Freewill offerings were given and a sanctuary tax was instituted (Ex. 30:12-16). They gave out of the abundance God blessed them with in their deliverance, when they spoiled the Egyptians (Ex. 12:36).

Weavers, metalworkers, and artists used their God-given skills to enhance worship and glorify God (Ex. 39:42). Two men commissioned by the Lord for such work were Bezaleel, the master artisan and perfumer responsible for mixing the sweet incense and holy oil and Aholiab the engraver (Ex. 35:30-35). This is a wonderful example of what it looks like to build a shared vision.

The Golden Altar

In Exodus 30:1, the Lord commands Moses, "and thou shalt make me an altar." This altar is different from the bronze altar found in the Outer Court, which was reserved for the burnt offerings and other sacrifices. Bronze in Scripture represents divine judgment.

The articles of worship in the Tabernacle are all types and symbols related to the Person and work of Christ, and to our position in relationship with Him. The Altar of Incense, a type of Christ our intercessor, is unique in its construction and significant in its placement.

> And thou shalt put it before the vail that is by the ark of the testimony, before the mercy seat that is over the testimony, where I will meet with thee.
>
> **Exodus 30:6**

This altar stood directly in front of the veil separating the ministering priests from the *Shekinah* above the Ark of the Covenant. The cloud of incense had to fill the place completely before the high priest could enter behind the veil annually on *Yom Kippur* (the Day of Atonement). What an awe-inspiring vision this gives us of God's glory and holiness, which should lead to a greater degree of the fear of the Lord!

> And Aaron shall make an atonement upon the horns of it once in a year with the blood of the sin offering of atonements: once in the year shall he make atonement upon it throughout your generations: it is most holy unto the LORD.
>
> EXODUS 30:10

Interestingly, the blood had to be applied to the altar to make atonement for it. Matthew Henry says this:

> The altar of incense represented the Son of God in his human nature, and the incense burned … typified his pleading for his people. The continual intercession of Christ was represented by the daily burning of incense… morning and evening. Once every year the blood of the atonement was to be applied to it, denoting that the intercession of Christ has all its virtue from his sufferings on earth, and that we need no other sacrifice or intercessor but Christ alone.[1]

It is striking that Christ makes up whatever may be lacking in the offerings we bring—He is for us, working all things together for our good (Rom. 8:26). John Wesley adds this:

> The prayers of saints are compared to sweet odours, but it is the incense which Christ adds to them that makes them acceptable; and his blood that atones for the guilt which cleaves to our best services.²

The real state of the heart before God and ability to offer true worship are connected. Our greatest offerings still need the cleansing blood to be applied. What a humbling thought! It is not what a person is on his or her own, but who Jesus Christ is in, through, and for them that makes the difference.

The altar was constructed with a crown around its top edge, which kept the hot coals and ash from falling to the ground. A similar crown could be found atop the Ark of the Covenant and Table of Showbread. It points to the royal or kingly position of Jesus Christ, as well as His priestly role. He sits on the throne, crowned with glory and honor (Heb. 2:9).

The horns of the altar represent spiritual power and authority, usually in connection with the anointing. Horns or shofars filled with oil were used to mark out God's choice of an individual for kingship or the prophetic office, as we see in the lives of David and Elisha (1 Sam. 16:13; 1 Kgs. 19:16). You can't just *go*, you have to be *sent*. It is God alone through His precious anointing that calls, confirms, separates, qualifies, and empowers for ministry!

This altar was also made of acacia (or shittim) wood. The wood was known for its strength, durability, and incorruptible nature, and is an appropriate type of the sinless human nature of Jesus Christ. Even in death, He did not see corruption (Acts 13:35-57; Rom. 6:9). This wood was entirely covered in gold, however, which is used to signify His deity or divine nature. Note that the two natures are pictured here as one piece, yet its elements are distinct from one another.

As we read about the Golden Altar and the incense, it is clear that God not only prescribes order, but He does it in great detail. Even the smallest aspect of the priest's duties and organization of the worship rituals was holy unto the Lord. Is today's church just as mindful of His involvement in the details of our worship and service?

INCENSE: AN ELEMENT OF WORSHIP

Many cultures commonly used incense in their worship rituals in biblical times. Some of the spices burned were also used for medicinal purposes. In the Tabernacle, the incense was an essential element of worship that illustrated heavenly truths. When Isaiah saw the Lord high and lifted up, he reported that "...the house was filled with smoke" (Isa. 6:1-4). John described a scene in heaven: "...golden vials full of odours, which are the prayers of saints" (Rev. 5:8). This three-dimensional imagery lets us know that God does not just "hear" prayer, but He "sees" the smoke and "smells" the fragrance!

The priests burned incense twice a day—morning and evening. This coincided with sacrifices, the trimming of the lamps, and the setting out of fresh bread. The incense in the sanctuary acted as a fumigant, offsetting the smell coming from the brazen altar in the Outer Court. This meant that the scent lingered all day and night. To "pray without ceasing" means keeping a prayerful spirit at all times (1 Th. 5:17).

On the Day of Atonement, when the high priest offered the special sacrifice and brought a portion of its blood into the Holy of Holies, he also carried incense in a golden censer (Lev. 16:12-13).

> And he shall take a censer full of burning coals of fire from off the altar before the LORD, and his hands full of sweet incense beaten small, and bring it within the vail: And he shall put the incense upon the fire before the LORD, that the cloud of the incense may cover the mercy seat that is upon the testimony, that he die not:
>
> **LEVITICUS 16:12-13**

Imagine the high priest's uneasiness as he enters the Holy of Holies! The cloud of perfume fills the entire tent (Lev. 16:13-14). Some believe the incense cloud shielded the high priest from gazing on the glory of God between the cherubim above the Ark; others see a prayer-covering, intervening to protect him from God's displeasure.[4] In any case, it is Christ's intercession alone that makes access to God's presence possible.

All other sources of fire were prohibited, as Nadab and Abihu discovered when they offered "strange fire" and were consumed—perhaps because the fire of the bronze altar of sacrifice had been ignited by God Himself (Lev. 9:24). The fire was holy, the altar holy, and the incense holy.

> Then Moses said unto Aaron, This is it that the LORD spake, saying, I will be sanctified in them that come nigh me, and before all the people I will be glorified. And Aaron held his peace.
>
> **LEVITICUS 10:3**

Not only were there prohibitions on the source of the fire, but on who could draw near to burn incense at the altar. Korah and his followers, who rebelled against the authority of Moses and Aaron, wanted to fill this office without having been appointed to it (Num. 16:1-5).

Dathan, Abiram, and many others were swallowed alive by the ground, and fire consumed those who offered incense—a sober reminder to honor God's delegated authorities and stay in one's lane of ministry (Num. 16:31-35). Aaron had to hurry to burn incense on the altar to make intercession for the people, who murmured against God's judgment after a plague broke out (Num. 16:46-50). The plague was stopped by intercession! He was a type of Christ, standing between the living and the dead (v. 48).

It is significant that at the opening of Luke's gospel, the priest Zacharias was chosen by lot to burn incense. After 400 years of silence from heaven, the angel Gabriel announced Messiah's coming.

He also announced His forerunner, John the Baptist, in answer to Zacharias's personal prayer for a child.

> And the whole multitude of the people were praying without at the time of incense. And there appeared unto him an angel of the Lord standing on the right side of the altar of incense.
>
> **LUKE 1:10-11**

Prayer is seen here as linked with prophecy and fulfillment. It connects our destiny with God's larger plan and purpose.

Its Composition

The sacred incense was a mixture of four different elements. This represents prayer, worship, and intercession. The priests worked together to gather what was needed, which brings to mind the saints helping to maintain the unity of the Spirit (Eph. 4:3). The composition of sweet spices commanded by God denotes divine grace. It is God adding His gifts and blessings to the works of His hands, in a kind of 4+1 arrangement.

This sweet aroma was unique to the service of God. No one was allowed to make this mixture to inhale it for their own enjoyment. The things of God are never there just for our entertainment, amusement, to be co-opted for other purposes, or to satisfy the curiosity of the natural or carnal man. What a lesson for today!

> And as for the perfume which thou shalt make, ye shall not make to yourselves according to the composition thereof: it shall be unto thee holy for the LORD. Whosoever shall make like unto that, to smell thereto, shall even be cut off from his people.
>
> **Exodus 30:37-38**

These ingredients not only appear here, but at other places in Scripture to confirm for us that there is nothing haphazard or incidental about God's plans and order.

> Then the LORD said to Moses, "Take for yourself spices, stacte and onycha and galbanum, spices with pure frankincense; there shall be an equal part of each. With it you shall make incense, a perfume, the work of a perfumer, salted, pure, and holy.
>
> **Exodus 30:34-35 NASB**

It is described as 1) fragrant, 2) salted, 3) pure, and 4) holy. Each ingredient was added in equal amount. Each was prepared separately, compounded into one mixture, and salted.

The first ingredient is *stacte*, which means "drops." It is "...the gum which spontaneously flows from the tree which produces myrrh."[5] It represents suffering and bitterness, especially in the crucifixion of Jesus. Myrrh appears at the beginning of Jesus' life as a gift from the wise men, and also at His death, when He is offered myrrh to drink, but refuses. It was also one of the principal spices used to prepare bodies for burial in biblical times. (See Matt. 2:11; Mark 15:23; and John 19:30) Further, the term "drops" may reference rain or perhaps water. Our prayers are to be like rain that is poured out on the earth. As rain is poured down, everyone can benefit from it—believers and non-believers. Myrrh will be discussed further in Chapter 7.

The second ingredient, *onycha*, comes from the exterior part (probably the claw) of a shell-fish in the Red Sea region. It was commonly used in the manufacture of ancient perfumes.[6] As the oil from this mollusk shell released a sweet odor, so our lives are become a channel through which the aroma of our prayer lives speak to all around us. It denotes one who is in touch with God. Interestingly, the Hebrew name of the shell, of obscure meaning, is derived from a root word meaning "to roar" or "a lion."[7] That is, there is a sound associated with this element—and worshipers know that there is always a "sound" that rings out in the midst of pure worship!

> There is always a "sound" that rings out in the midst of pure worship!

The third element, *galbanum*, was a "…resin of a pungent, bitter flavour, obtained by means of an incision in the bark, from the ferula, a shrub…and [is] then mixed with fragrant substances to give greater pungency to their odour."[8] It enhances the scents of other spices it is mixed with, but is unpleasant on it's own. This speaks of hardship and trial that makes the grace of God in us more evident. This spice was also used to prevent or relieve spasms (a sudden, abnormal, or involuntary contraction of the muscle). Believers must grow in such depth as to response to life's sudden changes with prayer for guidance and direction, ever trusting God to bring us through in victory. In its more intense form, it could be a signal that a more intense spiritual warfare is needed to remain steadfast.

The fourth ingredient was a white tree resin called *frankincense*, very common in Scripture for its pleasing aroma. Like myrrh, we find it presented to Jesus as a young Child. The frankincense was said to be "pure," and points to the purity of Christ. White speaks of His perfect righteousness. It possesses an element of mystery to it, as *The Biblical Illustrator* brings out:

> Frankincense, when burned, "…sends up sweet clouds to the sky. It is the symbol of religious thought directing itself lovingly and longingly towards God. It typifies what is inward. There is a life of contemplation as well as of action.[9]

Finally, this mixture was compounded and then seasoned with salt. Salt is a preservative against corruption but also has the added benefit of enhancing usefulness and flavor. Why salt in the offering of prayer and worship? Salt represents grace that keeps down the advance of sin's corruption in our lives. Good, gracious, kind, and beneficial speech is said to be "seasoned with salt" (Col. 4:6; Jas. 3:10, 12). There is a danger of salt becoming ineffective in its purpose.

> For every one shall be salted with fire, and every sacrifice shall be salted with salt. Salt is good: but if the salt have lost his saltness, wherewith will ye season it? Have salt in yourselves, and have peace one with another.
>
> **MARK 9:49-50**

Salt is also related to covenant, perfection, and purity, and was required to be present in all of the burnt offerings (Lev. 2:13).

Note that the elements of the incense were beaten small. In some cases, the bark had to be cut first. Everything that will be used by God endures a process of transformation that makes it suitable for His purposes. Many want to flow in greater degrees of anointing, but not many want to pay the cost. The process is not pleasant—there is a beating, a pounding, and a crushing that takes place. Usefulness requires transformation.

Usefulness requires transformation.

This brings to mind the sufferings of Christ. In Gethsemane, the place of the olive press, He wrestled in prayer. He also endured physical sufferings and carried the weight of our sins. He "humbled Himself" and "learned obedience" by the things He went through. It was painful, but at the end, the sweet fragrance of submission to the Father's will was released.

And being in an agony he prayed more earnestly: and his sweat was as it were great drops of blood falling down to the ground.

LUKE 22:44-45

...that he by the grace of God should taste death for every man. For it became him... to make the captain of their salvation perfect through sufferings.

HEBREWS 2:9-10

...Christ also hath loved us, and hath given himself for us an offering and a sacrifice to God for a sweet-smelling savour.

EPHESIANS 5:2

None of the ingredients for the incense could produce the aroma God required on its own or in its natural state. He doesn't leave us in our natural condition, but brings us into His sanctification process to purify and set us apart. (Sanctification cannot be separated from the anointing.) It is powerful when a congregation can unite in expressions of pure worship. It takes all of us working together, experiencing and expanding the kingdom of God.

HELP US, HOLY SPIRIT

The Word of God encourages us to pray in the name of Jesus, pray in the Spirit, and pray in faith and humility. It's not just *saying* the name of Jesus, it's the power of our living relationship with Him that makes the difference. No one prays "perfectly." We are in constant need of God's help.

> Likewise the Spirit also helpeth our infirmities: for we know not what we should pray for as we ought: but the Spirit itself maketh intercession for us with groanings which cannot be uttered…
>
> …It is Christ that died, yea rather, that is risen again, who is even at the right hand of God, who also maketh intercession for us.
>
> **ROMANS 8:26, 34**

The Holy Spirit pleads for us out of divine omniscience, bypassing our human emotions and limitations. Our shortcomings in prayer do not keep us from obtaining the answer, for the Holy Spirit is there to help, making our prayers what they ought to be (1 John 5:14). I should note that one can be emotional without being spiritual, but if one is truly spiritual, the emotions will be touched as well.

David understood something when he compared prayer and worship to incense and sacrifice. He was saying, "Lord, let it be pleasing in your sight."

> LORD, I cry unto thee: make haste unto me; give ear unto my voice, when I cry unto thee. Let my prayer be set forth before thee as incense; and the lifting up of my hands as the evening sacrifice.
>
> **PSALMS 141:1-2**

> And another angel came and stood at the altar, having a golden censer; and there was given unto him much incense, that he should offer it with the prayers of all saints upon the Golden Altar which was before the throne. And the smoke of the incense, which came with the prayers of the saints, ascended up before God out of the angel's hand. And the angel took the censer, and filled it with fire of the altar, and cast it into the earth: and there were voices, and thunderings, and lightnings, and an earthquake.
>
> **REVELATION 8:3-5**

Prayers are everlasting and impact the universal course of events. Our praise and worship is also received by the Lord as a sweet-smelling sacrifice. As the true Altar of Incense, Jesus Christ is the *means by which* these offerings are properly presented before God. He sanctifies the gifts offered by Him (Matt. 23:19).

> <u>By him</u> therefore let us offer the sacrifice of praise to God continually, that is, the fruit of our lips giving thanks to his name.
>
> **HEBREWS 13:15**

Praise must be continual, not depending on how one feels at the moment. There are only two times to praise Him: when you feel like it, and when you don't! There's always something to be thankful for. Because of who Jesus is, petitions made in His name and by the power of the Spirit will always be accepted—and prevail.

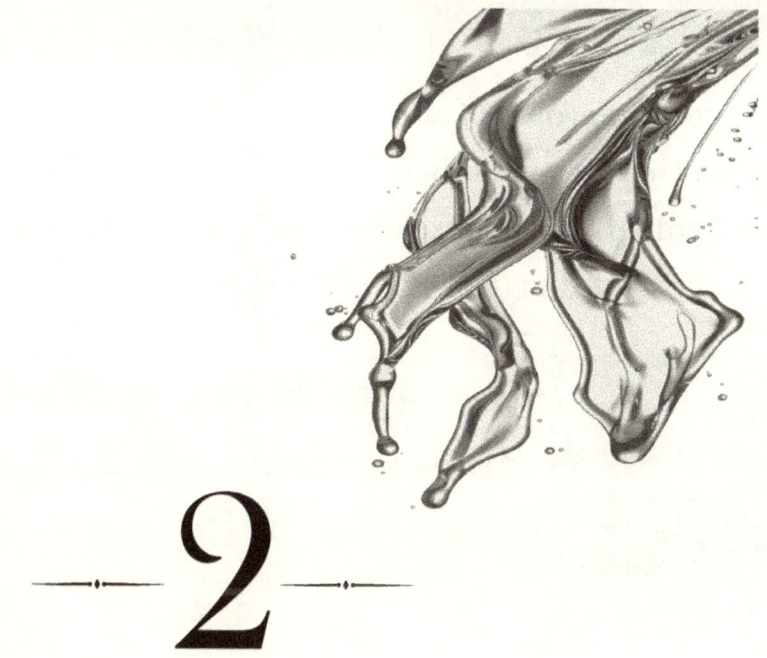

2

Prayer and Intercession

Through Jesus Christ, we can have an audience with God—privately and corporately. It is the essence of our relationship with God. Prayer doesn't hit the ceiling and fall back on us—it ascends as a sweet savor before the throne of grace. We can petition God to bring His will to pass on earth, as it is in heaven. We can intercede for others, to bring down the blessing. The apostle Paul understood this, and prayed for believers as often as he requested their prayers on his behalf.

Anyone who has read or just heard the Bible mentioned will agree that "prayer" abounds in hundreds of places, events and in the lives of many people. One of the earliest mentions of prayer is recorded in Genesis 4:26, when "…men began to call on the name of the Lord." This action continues right up to the culmination of history as recorded in the Book of Revelation.

> Your posture is one of trust and obedience; God's posture is one of extending His mercy and grace.

For believers today, prayer is still one's lifeblood. It must never be a spare tire; it must be the steering wheel of your life (Corrie Ten Boom). Prayer becomes an exchange between you and God; a dialogue. Your posture is one of trust and obedience; God's posture is one of extending His mercy and grace. Prayer not only changes things; it changes the person who prays.

How well I remember my godly parents who taught and modeled before me how to pray. I recall a day when, as a young teenager, my mother fell ill with intestinal cancer and was given a very limited time to live. My father agonized in prayer through the late hours of the night and early morning, usually when the family was sleeping. After some period of time he announced to the family that she would be raised from that sickness and outlive him. More than thirty years had passed since that word was received in prayer! It happened just as he spoke and believed it.

This example set at home was a powerful teaching tool that has kept me motivated and focused until this day. The "all night prayer meetings" of my youth have also impacted and elevated my faith and confidence in the word of the Lord.

What is prayer? As the Greek verb *proseuchomai*, it is simply talking to God.[1] There are various types of prayer, including: petition or supplication, confession, travail, thanksgiving, and intercession. Prayer also includes expressions of praise, adoration, and communion. Spiritual warfare adds another dimension. A vibrant prayer life is a key to victory and growth.

Prayer accesses God's presence, which transforms us. Do you have a set time daily for talking to the Lord? It is a two-way conversation, not a monologue. We can bring all of our needs and concerns to Him. But part of worship involves waiting on the Lord, who gives guidance and direction as we seek to know His will.

All of the types, shadows, and figures of the Old Covenant were representations of the realities we experience under the New Covenant. Prayer works the faith that is the essence of our new spiritual life. It's grounded in God's promises, not a leap in the dark or wishful thinking.

> For therein is the righteousness of God revealed from faith to faith: as it is written, The just shall live by faith.
>
> **ROMANS 1:17**

How would you say your prayer life is growing? And where should you begin if you are just starting out? Apostle Paul gives us a list of people we can intercede for, and the kinds of prayer we can use.

> I exhort therefore, that, first of all, supplications, prayers, intercessions, and giving of thanks, be made for all men; For kings, and for all that are in authority; that we may lead a quiet and peaceable life in all godliness and honesty.
>
> **1 Timothy 2:1-2**

> Praying always with all prayer and supplication in the Spirit, and watching thereunto with all perseverance and supplication for all saints; And for me, that utterance may be given unto me, that I may open my mouth boldly, to make known the mystery of the gospel.
>
> **Ephesians 6:18-19**

These verses give us categories of prayer requests. Note the order: 1) all people everywhere, 2) leaders of nations, 3) all authority figures, 4) a quiet and peaceful life for believers, 5) all saints everywhere, and 6) leaders in the body of Christ, in their respective places. Ministers need divine boldness and expression to preach the gospel. Prayer actively seeks this blessing for them. There is much to pray for!

There are some things that just won't happen without prayer. God accomplishes His will through the prayers of the saints! Very often we receive blessing as the fruit of someone else's labor. Those connected to us may be unaware of our cries before the throne on their behalf. We can plead for answers to every pressing need. God's church is a praying church! Great moves of God are always birthed in prayer before they are manifested in the open.

Note: there is one thing that contributes to spiritual progress which is beyond any scientific or man-made exercise. That something is the combination of fasting and prayer. The ultimate goal of this discipline is to exalt and please Jesus Christ as Lord.

> Delight yourself in the Lord and He shall give you the desires of your heart.
>
> **PSALM 37:4**

Spiritually, the acts of fasting and prayer release one's energy to become effective in his or her God-given assignment. The practice of fasting and prayer is a cornerstone of the Christian faith and one of the pillars of other religions. Fasting and prayer will release one from the bondage of unbelief and allow the inner man to be a conduit of supernatural power.

In the gospel narratives of Matthew, Mark, and Luke, a distressed father brought his young son, who suffered from epileptic seizures, to the disciples for healing. As it turned out, "they could not cure him" (Matt. 17:14-16). As a convulsion came upon the boy, Jesus rebuked the demonic spirit, taking his hand and delivering him to his father. This demonstrated His work of healing and grace. After this miracle the disciples asked the Lord why they could not cast the evil spirit out (v. 17-19).

Jesus declared that it was *because of their unbelief*. He also clarified that some works of healing can only be accomplished through prayer and fasting (Matt. 17:0-21). Although this was a stinging phrase, it emphasized two great needs: the power of faith and the intercession and self-denial that accompany these disciplines.

Interesting, there were those who attempted (or pretended) to accomplish deliverance in the name of Jesus who were not linked Christ at all. In the absence of true faith, they were beat and humiliated before the enemy (Acts 19:13-17).

Intercession

In the Bible, an intercessor is someone who stands in the gap between God and others. Job wished for a mediator to stand between he and God to present his case (Job 9:33). In the Old Testament, prophets and priests interceded for the people with God. The gap represents sin and its damaging effects. Jesus Christ has come as the only mediator between God and humanity, and our Great High Priest (1 Tim. 2:5).

> I looked for a man among them who would build up the wall and stand before me in the gap on behalf of the land so I would not have to destroy it, but I found none.
>
> **Ezekiel 22:30**

Intercession is still needed today—it is pleading with God on behalf of another person. It is wrestling in prayer to bring down the blessing and see the promise fulfilled. There may be times when people may be unable or unwilling to pray for themselves, or unaware of their own need. Intercession is rooted in revelation. Interesting, God isn't just seeking worshippers, He's also looking for intercessors!

For example, when Daniel understood from reading the writings of Jeremiah that the time of Israel's captivity was almost over, he turned to prayer and fasting: confession, supplication, and intercession. It was God revealing His plans in advance to His servants the prophets (Amos 3:7). Knowing God's promises, one can pray accordingly. There is a link between the prophetic and intercessory prayer. However, one may have a prophetic temperament, and not be a prophet. Intercessory prayer is also connected to divine timing.

> We yet need committed prayer partners who will intercede, trusting God for His kingdom to be advanced.

Jesus taught His disciples how to pray by precept and example. But in John 17, He interceded for the disciples and all who would come to faith as a result of their ministry. This is often called His high-priestly prayer. The risen, glorified Christ lives forever to intercede for us. The Holy Spirit also intercedes for us with groanings! God's got you covered! (Rom. 8:26, 34).

The Apostle Paul makes his request in 2 Thessalonians 3:1 with the statement: "Finally, brethren, pray for us, that the word of the Lord may have free course and be glorified, even as it is with you." The translation of "pray" means to pray continually. In this day, we yet need committed prayer partners who will intercede and trust God for the kingdom of God to be advanced again and again!

Spirit-filled believers are called to cover each other in prayer. Corporate prayer has its own dynamic. Sometimes you've got to find an agreer to get the breakthrough. God's presence is there, wherever two or three are gathered in His name (Matt. 18:19-20). Pray until something happens!

Abraham Intercedes

The Lord let the patriarch Abraham know that He would destroy the cities of Sodom and Gomorrah, the place where Abraham's nephew, Lot, had settled, because of their wickedness. What Abraham did next is an example of intercessory prayer, the first prayer of its kind in the Bible. It shows God's mercy in hearing the petitions of His people.

> Abraham came near and said, "Will You indeed sweep away the righteous with the wicked? Suppose there are fifty righteous within the city; will You indeed sweep it away and not spare the place for the sake of the fifty righteous who are in it? Far be it from You to do such a thing, to slay

the righteous with the wicked, so that the righteous and the wicked are treated alike. Far be it from You! Shall not the Judge of all the earth deal justly?"

Genesis 18:23-25 NASB

Abraham petitioned God based on His character—He knew God was the righteous judge. He looked for a way that the city could be spared, but respected the judgment of God in the situation. When he had prayed so that God was willing to spare the city if there were ten righteous within it, there came an end to his requests. Abraham prayed and sought God's compassion.

Prayer gives reasons, make requests, and claims promises. It involves persistence and faith. Abraham kept asking; he didn't give up easily. Does this sound familiar?

> And I say unto you, Ask, and it shall be given you; seek, and ye shall find; knock, and it shall be opened unto you. For every one that asketh receiveth; and he that seeketh findeth; and to him that knocketh it shall be opened.
>
> **Luke 11:9-10**

> …The effectual fervent prayer of a righteous man availeth much.
>
> **James 5:16**

Everyone needs prayer…friends, enemies, leaders. When people ask for prayer, do you really remember to pray for them? Don't let "I'm praying for you" become a cliché without a commitment. In fact, restraining prayer or neglecting prayer is also sin. Samuel recognized this when it came to praying for the Israelites who had chosen Saul as their king. When they asked for his prayers, he responded:

> Moreover as for me, God forbid that I should sin against the LORD in ceasing to pray for you: but I will teach you the good and the right way:
>
> 1 SAMUEL 12:23

Yes, they would have his intercession, but they also had his warning to remain faithful to the Lord, which he would teach them to do.

STRANGE FIRE ON THE ALTAR!

This is a good place to revisit the matter of Nadab and Abihu.

> Now Nadab and Abihu, the sons of Aaron, took their respective firepans, and after putting fire in them, placed incense on it and offered strange fire before the Lord, which He had not commanded them. And fire came out from the presence of the Lord and consumed them, and they died before the Lord.
>
> LEVITICUS 10:1-2 NASB

Nadab and Abihu were Aaron's eldest sons who served at the altar. They had the rare privilege of accompanying Moses up Mount Sinai where "they saw the God of Israel," in a manifestation that is not detailed (Ex. 24:10). They saw Moses go up into the mount to receive the Ten Commandments, yet they were either careless or presumptuous in burning the holy incense.

These two young men died right where they stood. I'm sure the other priests took note to carry out their duties according to the pattern, and not to intrude into holy things with "innovation." It is as shocking as the case of Ananias and Sapphira, which also served as an object lesson to the early church.[2]

A careful study reveals that what happened here was like someone being struck by lightning, by fire that came from the midst of the sanctuary. This is because neither their garments nor bodies were consumed, and yet they died.[3] What exactly did they do to provoke such a swift response from the presence of the Lord?

The most common thought is that they used fire other than God's fire to light the incense. Whatever it was, it was something God never authorized. Consider the following parallel drawn by Alexander MacLaren:

> How much so-called Christian worship glows with self-will or with partisan zeal! When we seek to worship God for what we can get, when we rush into His presence with hot, eager desires which we have not subordinated to His will, we are burning 'strange fire which He has not commanded.' The only fire which should kindle the incense in our censers, and send it up to heaven in fragrant

wreaths, is fire caught from the altar of sacrifice. God must kindle the flame in our hearts…[4]

Obviously, sincerity alone is not enough. There is a prescribed order. Disobedience is costly!

> Wherefore we receiving a kingdom which cannot be moved, let us have grace, whereby we may serve God acceptably with reverence and godly fear: For our God is a consuming fire.
>
> **HEBREWS 12:28-29**

MOTIVES AND ATTITUDES IN PRAYER

The altar of prayer is the place for expression of relationship, requests, and claiming God's promises. But sin and impure motives can hinder prayer. It's not just how one asks, but what one asks for and why one asks for it, that matters. The Spirit leads to repentance through conviction (not condemnation!), so you can ask and receive with fullness of joy.

> If I regard iniquity in my heart, the Lord will not hear me:
> **PSALMS 66:18**

> Ye ask, and receive not, because ye ask amiss, that ye may consume it upon your lusts.
>
> **JAMES 4:3**

> And this is the confidence that we have in him, that, if we ask any thing according to his will, he heareth us: And if we know that he hear us, whatsoever we ask, we know that we have the petitions that we desired of him.
>
> 1 John 5:14-15

God's ear is open to the cry of the righteous (Ps. 34:15). Secret prayer will be rewarded openly in due season (Matt. 6:5-7).

Note that part of the proper attitude in prayer is answering the call to forgiveness of any who have wronged us. Refusal to forgive offenders—from the heart, and not merely in pretense—is one of the greatest hindrances to effective prayer.

> But I say unto you, Love your enemies, bless them that curse you, do good to them that hate you, and pray for them which despitefully use you, and persecute you;
>
> Matthew 5:44

> And when ye stand praying, forgive, if ye have ought against any: that your Father also which is in heaven may forgive you your trespasses.
>
> Mark 11:25

We will find it easier to forgive those who have sinned against us when we remember how much the Father has forgiven us! It is good to call to mind the personal mercies we have received, the great love that was manifested at the cross, and be willing to extend that love and grace toward others! This is a mark of spiritual maturity, and an essential element of our faith-walk with Jesus.

The New Testament sheds more light on the connection of prayer to the incense of God.

> Be ye therefore followers of God as dear children; and walk in love, as Christ also loved us, and hath given Himself for us an offering and a sacrifice to God for a sweet smelling savor.
>
> **EPHESIANS 5:1-2**

> Now thanks be to God, which always causes us to triumph in Christ and maketh manifest the savor of His knowledge by us in every place. For we are unto God a sweet savor of Christ, in them that are saved and in them that perish.
>
> **2 CORINTHIANS 2:14-15**

What a comparison! What is actually released? It is the sweet smell of the gifts, graces, and glories of the Holy Spirit. It is not the flesh that produces this fragrance, but the life of Christ. Think of Aaron and his sons when the aromatic anointing oil was poured on their heads and ran to their garment's edge.[5] The incense of prayer and the oil of God are linked. Where there is one, the other will be.

It doesn't take any special kind of person to pray. Because of Jesus Christ, we can "…come boldly unto the throne of grace" where mercy and help is available whenever we need it (Heb. 4:16). In prayer, surrender and brokenness meet boldness and access. Faith combines with humility and trust. When you dialogue with God, you are starting in the right place!

When the sweet incense ascends from our lives, we will display sweetness, holiness, purity, and give off the aroma of life leading to life. But the presence of salt will also be evident. This means demonstrating grace, humility, and self-control. Having peace with one another means not being contentious, being divisive, cliquish, or anything that gives a bad "taste." In other words, no nonsense, no craziness, no foolishness. It is behaving oneself wisely. Acknowledge Him in all your ways…clarity and direction will come.

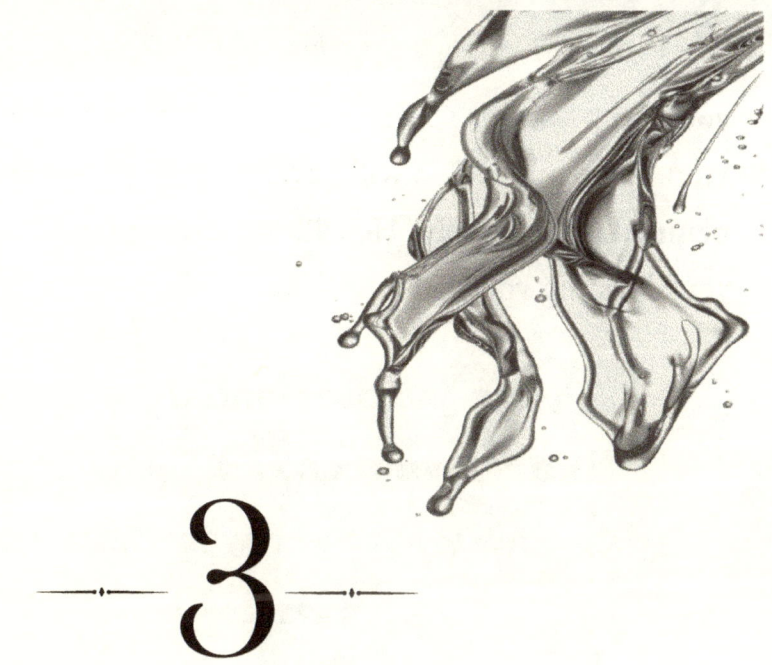

3

From Blessing to Presence

*T*his is a study on elements of the true anointing and its overflow. We now understand that God desires to live in our midst, but that His worship and our service comes with certain requirements and postures. The Altar of Incense, the censer, and the fragrance that arises before God have encouraged us to pursue a lifestyle of prayer and worship. We also understand the heart attitudes necessary for effective prayer, and the role of intercessors in the church.

The presence of God causes us to pray in the Spirit to get the mind of the Father. God's presence *within* you puts things in check *around* you and positions you to engage and contend for the promises of God. Remember, God will never let you go in if He has not already planned your way out. He will not steer you where He has not seen you elevating your faith.

> *Your purpose must be greater than your conflict; your spiritual influence greater than your resistance.*

In kingdom assignments and prophetic birthing, God will push you to places without your permission because He speaks out of His glory (presence). You will understand that you are chosen. Jeremiah was persecuted and arrested. He did not make that choice, the choice was made for him. Your purpose must be greater than your conflict; your spiritual influence greater than your resistance. You must put the past in perspective and settle on the present and future.

The word *blessing* carries the idea of speaking well of something or someone. This really means celebrating God with praises, as well as kneeling in adoration. This means that one acknowledges His goodness with a desire for His glory (presence). The word describes something that is pleasurable or wonderful or good. By contrast, *presence* signifies JEHOVAH-SHAMMAH declaring "the Lord is there." (Ezek. 48:35). This denotes the fact that God rests "there" with all the blessings, peace, security, and glory of His abiding presence.

Don't just pursue the blessings of God (His goodness and benefits), but desire His presence. When His presence is "there," everything else will be added (Matt. 6:33).

Life is a unique mixture of both good and bad, bitter and sweet, ups and downs, sunshine and rain. These elements make up what the Apostle Paul calls the "all things" that work together for our good (Rom. 8:26). Those who read and believe what God says in His Word will not go through life as troubled over circumstances and events as others. In short, spiritual things must be spiritually discerned, and together with your perception of biblical truths, intimacy with God is inevitable.

In light of this, we can consider the anointing of God. Many want the anointing, but what does that really mean? It is one thing to want God to do something for us, quite another to walk daily in the conscious awareness of His nearness, and operate out of that reality in the miraculous as well as the mundane. Having the presence of the Lord, we actually have enough—and more than enough!

Spirituality

The word *spirit* is defined in Scripture as the "breath" or "wind." The two main Hebrew words for this are *rûach* and *neshâmâh*. The Greek equivalent is the word *pneuma*. The terms often appear together, usually related to movement, impartation, or expiration. We did not make ourselves, and we are not self-sustaining (Ps. 100:3;

Eccl. 8:8).

In creation, the breath of the Almighty gives life (Job 33:4). The Spirit moves as the wind, unseen but felt, and brings about the new birth (John 3:8). Ezekiel prophesied to the breath in the Valley of Dry Bones (Ezek. 37:9), and the breath of God is also linked to the writing of Scripture (2 Tim. 3:16). The Greek term for *inspiration* is actually "God-breathed." God's judgment on the wicked is also described as the releasing of His breath against them (Isa. 11:4; 2 Thess. 2:8).

Our life is compared to a vapor that's only here for a moment, and then vanishes (Jas. 4:14). When the spirit leaves the body, our frames return to the dust from which they came (Gen. 3:19; Ps. 104:29). This is sobering, and teaches us to number our days. What a powerful truth! God creates time, cuts out a space of that time, blows His breath upon that time, and that is our life!

Consider the progression of the Bible's teaching on the Spirit, the wind, and the breath of God in the following seven verses:

> And the Spirit of God moved upon the face of the waters.
>
> **GENESIS 1:2**

> And the LORD God…breathed into his nostrils the breath of life; and man became a living soul.
>
> **GENESIS 2:7**

Then shall the dust return to the earth as it was: and the spirit shall return unto God who gave it.

ECCLESIASTES 12:7

The wind bloweth where it listeth, and thou hearest the sound thereof, but canst not tell whence it cometh, and whither it goeth: so is every one that is born of the Spirit.

JOHN 3:8

And when he had said this, he breathed on them, and saith unto them, Receive ye the Holy Ghost.

JOHN 20:22

…Father, into thy hands I commend my spirit: and having said thus, he gave up the ghost.

LUKE 23:46

And suddenly there came a sound from heaven as of a rushing mighty wind, and it filled all the house…

ACTS 2:2

We live, move, and have our being because of God (Acts 17:28). Natural breath animates us and activates our consciousness and life (Rom. 14:12; 2 Cor. 5:10). Animals also live by the breath of God, but are not God-conscious (Eccl. 3:21). If you have breath in your body and are connected in relationship, you are commanded to praise the Lord (Ps. 150:6). God's people ought to *breathe* His praise!

Cain was held accountable for taking the life of his brother, Abel, whose name actually meant breath, vapor, or vanity. Jesus told the story of the Rich Fool whose soul was "required of him" in one night (Luke 12:20).

> So then every one of us shall give account of himself to God.
> **ROMANS 14:12**

> For we must all appear before the judgment seat of Christ…
> **2 CORINTHIANS 5:10**

We are accountable for the anointing as well. The Holy Spirit gives us a new nature capable of displaying Christ's character (Eph. 4:24). This produces real change in a person's life—making him or her a "partaker of the divine nature" (2 Pet. 1:4). In other words, the Holy Spirit produces a holy people. It means we are living, loving, and growing together in kingdom relationships (Heb. 13:17; 1 Pet. 5:5). Submission is a part of this. The anointing is also administrated in the ways we relate to the state, our family, and our work.

HOLINESS

The Greek word for holiness is *hagiōsunē*, and it means "sacredness."[1] Sacredness implies devotion and distinction—to be set apart. God is holy, and calls His children to holiness (1 Pet. 1:15-16). A believer's life will be marked by a demonstration of Christ's character. There will be a desire to "[perfect] holiness in the fear of God" (2 Cor. 7:1).

He has given us everything we need for life and godliness (2 Pet. 1:3). Holiness is not a list of dos and don'ts rooted in tradition.

There is a need for constant cleansing from anything that would defile our bodies or spirits (1 Pet. 1:15). His ultimate goal in us is conformity to the image of Jesus Christ (Rom. 8:29; 1 Jn. 3:2). We move from one level of faith, strength, and glory to another, according to His timing and purpose. Self-examination is an important part of the process.

The prophet Isaiah was confronted by God's holiness. The angels cried, "Holy, holy, holy, is the LORD of hosts: the whole earth is full of his glory" (Isa. 6:3). Note that a confrontation with the holiness of God also means a confrontation with one's own sinfulness. The first thing he cried was, "Woe is me, for I am undone!" (Isa. 6:5) But he didn't get stuck there—he received cleansing from the altar and a renewed calling.

Moses also encountered God's presence in the burning bush:

> And Moses said, I will now turn aside, and see this great sight, why the bush is not burnt. And when the LORD saw that he turned aside to see, God called unto him out of the midst of the bush, and said, Moses, Moses. And he said, Here am I. And he said, Draw not nigh hither: put off thy shoes from off thy feet, for the place whereon thou standest is holy ground.
>
> **EXODUS 3:3-5**

First, Moses turned aside to see. God draws us to Himself (Isa. 30:21; John 6:44). Many times people say, "I've found God," but really it is God who finds us and reveals our destiny in Him. When God shows up it is a "crisis" moment. There is an interruption. He went out of his way to get a fuller picture. Revelation led to illumination which changed his destination and led to a greater understanding of his purpose. Don't burn yourself out trying to create a purpose—turn aside to encounter God's presence to discover it. And there is always more to discover!

> May be able to comprehend with all saints what is the breadth, and length, and depth, and height; And to know the love of Christ, which passeth knowledge, that ye might be filled with all the fulness of God.
>
> **EPHESIANS 3:18-19**

Second, God called to Moses, and he responded. God always speaks first. It was true with Adam in the Garden of Eden (Gen. 3:9), the young prophet Samuel (1 Sam. 3:4), and Saul of Tarsus (Acts 9:4). The question is, do we recognize when God speaking? We must be attuned to His voice; we must be quiet enough (for long enough) to hear His instruction. When God calls, we must answer with a yes! And after that yes, give God another yes!

> And when he putteth forth his own sheep, he goeth before them, and the sheep follow him: for they know his voice.
>
> **JOHN 10:4**

Third, Moses was told to keep a safe or proper distance from the burning bush—in other words, to respond to God's presence with an attitude of reverence. The ground was considered holy because the presence of God was being manifested there. The Israelites were told to keep a distance Mount Sinai, lest they die (Ex. 19:11-13). Recall that the high priest was not allowed to enter the Holy of Holies except on the Day of Atonement (Heb. 9:7). Although we now have free access to God through Jesus Christ, beware of becoming too "familiar" or careless in His presence (Eccl. 5:1-5).

> Draw nigh to God, and he will draw nigh to you. Cleanse your hands, ye sinners; and purify your hearts, ye double minded.
>
> **JAMES 4:8**

Finally, Moses had to remove his shoes. In Bible times, it was customary to remove one's sandals before entering a home, for they had picked up the filth of the world and would track the dirt indoors. A considerate host would provide water for guests to wash their feet.

> That ye put off concerning the former conversation the old man, which is corrupt according to the deceitful lusts.
>
> **EPHESIANS 4:22**

> But now ye also put off all these; anger, wrath, malice, blasphemy, filthy communication out of your mouth. Lie not one to another, seeing that ye have put off the old man with his deeds.
>
> **COLOSSIANS 3:8-9**

As it is in the spiritual, so it is in the natural. We are called to "put off" that which does not please God, removing anything that would hinder the flow of the Spirit in and through us.

Anointing

What exactly is the anointing? The term *anointing* refers to the act of rubbing or smearing with oil, for religious or medicinal reasons.[2] This represents the Holy Spirit, and relates to power, presence, grace and strength. Power in this sense is both authoritative and dynamic. It flows through us, enabling us to fulfill our kingdom assignment. It comes to "do" something in your life and the lives of those around you.

There is a connection between the words *anointed* and *consecrated*. The first mention of the words *anoint* and *consecrate* appear in the book of Exodus, and relate to the installation of Aaron and his sons into the priestly office (Ex. 28:3, 41). Consecration referred to someone or something being completely sanctified, appointed, or even pronounced clean. It is "to separate from profane things and dedicate to God," but also "to purify internally by renewing of the soul."[3]

There are several Hebrew and Greek words rendered anointed or anointing. Here are a few:

Hebrew Words

yitshâr — oil as used to produce light

shemen — grease (liquid) from perfumed olive oil; conveys the idea of richness and fruitfulness

mimshach — to rub, smear, or spread, with the thought of expansion or being outspread[4]

Greek Words

epichriō — to smear over

murizō — to apply perfumed or medicinal ointment

chriō — to rub with oil; implies consecration to an office [5]

The anointing with oil is also linked to prayers of faith by the elders for deliverance and recovery from sickness (Jas. 5:14). Jesus anoints believers with the Spirit, enabling them to live holy lives, perform acts of power, and walk in various ministries (Acts 2:33). Obviously, He possesses the Spirit without measure (John 3:34). The title "Christ," is derived from the Greek word *christos*, meaning "Anointed One."

This anointing is our source of spiritual life and effectiveness. In fact, we are commanded to be filled with the Spirit (Eph. 5:18). But the anointing comes from God alone, and is not man-made. It has a "formula," and "ingredients" as we learn through the incense and the anointing oil, that can't be duplicated, bought, sold, controlled, or concocted artificially. It is real, genuine, and authentic.

All believers have some measure of the anointing—but to live out its fullness is a process of maturation and sanctification.

> Wherefore I give you to understand, that no man speaking by the Spirit of God calleth Jesus accursed: and that no man can say that Jesus is the Lord, but by the Holy Ghost.
>
> **1 Corinthians 12:3**

> But ye are not in the flesh, but in the Spirit, if so be that the Spirit of God dwell in you. Now if any man have not the Spirit of Christ, he is none of his.
>
> **Romans 8:9**

One must move away from just emotional excitement and spectatorship into accessing and dwelling in the presence of the Lord. This is not a momentary touch that fails to produce real change over time. A desire for His presence is about seeking the face and heart of God. Remember what the Holy Spirit comes to do!

In the Gospel of John 14:16-17 we read:

> And I will pray the Father, and he shall give you another Comforter, that he may abide with you for ever; Even the Spirit of truth…ye know him; for he dwelleth with you, and shall be in you.
>
> **John 14:16-17**

In the Old Testament, God's acts of power were manifested by the Spirit, or the anointing, coming upon men and women to perform specific tasks. It was a power acting on Him "from without," if you will.

> And the Spirit of the LORD came mightily upon him, and he rent him as he would have rent a kid, and he had nothing in his hand...
>
> **JUDGES 14:6**

> Then Samuel took the horn of oil, and anointed him... and the Spirit of the LORD came upon David from that day forward...
>
> **1 SAMUEL 16:13**

In the New Testament, we see something new and powerful taking place. The church becomes the true Tabernacle of God (Eph. 2:22).

> These all continued with one accord in prayer and supplication...And there appeared unto them cloven tongues like as of fire, and it sat upon each of them. And they were all filled with the Holy Ghost, and began to speak with other tongues, as the Spirit gave them utterance.
>
> **ACTS 1:14 & 2:3-4**

Observe the incense of prayer, the purifying fire of God, and the flow of praise that followed! Treasure was poured into earthen vessels and Christ's character was evident. They followed the apostle's doctrine and much fruit followed (Acts 2:42). They experienced love, joy, boldness, faith, generosity, and power because of the anointing. We can experience the same blessing and presence today. Hallelujah!

Jesus was speaking figuratively of the Holy Spirit when He said:

> …If any man thirst, let him come unto me, and drink. He that believeth on me, as the scripture hath said, out of *his* belly shall flow rivers of living water. (But this spake he of the Spirit, which they that believe on him should receive: for the Holy Ghost was not yet given; because that Jesus was not yet glorified.)
>
> **JOHN 7:38-39**

It is crucial that one understands the entire context of this verse. The invitation, "if any man thirst, let him come to Me and drink," actually means he (the person who believes on Jesus), let him drink. However, the words "his belly" in verse 38 do not refer to the believer at all, but to Jesus Christ! The person is Himself, pointing to Jesus as the giver. He is the source of all spiritual blessing, as "the scripture hath said" (Isa. 12:3, 55:1; Joel 3:18). Then in verse 39, the interpretation is clearly given: "…but this spake He of the Spirit, which they that believe on Him should receive…" Jesus is the giver and the believer is the receiver!

Having established this, "flow" is understood as an action that comes "through" and not originated "by" the believer. The expression "flowing with the flow" then means *moving with God as He speaks and directs through the Holy Spirit.*

If that is the flow, what is the overflow? It suggests an abundance, a flood or deluge of something. Paul describes such an experience when he said, "Great is my boldness of speech toward you, great is my glorying of you; I am filled with comfort, I am exceeding joyful in all our tribulation" (2 Cor. 7:4). What a blessed state of maturity to have an abundance of joy in the midst of the challenges and changes life can bring.

> *You can have an abundance of joy in the midst of the challenges and changes life can bring.*

Things were not always easy for the first believers. Persecution broke out and their lives were endangered. But they had the flow and the overflow, and the seed of the Word was scattered wherever they went! (Acts 8:4). The anointing will make you an overcomer!

> We are troubled on every side, yet not distressed; we are perplexed, but not in despair; Persecuted, but not forsaken; cast down, but not destroyed.
>
> 2 CORINTHIANS 4:8-9

Remember why you are where you are in the present season. Your words and life can be salt and light in your circle of influence. God positions us to bring glory to His awesome name and advance the kingdom, not private agendas. Some are seed-sowers, some are waterers, but the increase and the glory belong to God.

Becoming powerful in the kingdom becomes a corporate investment strategy. It's what the team does over the long haul, day by day that really matters. Making the shift means waging a good warfare (1 Tim. 1:18). Obedience, faith, commitment and partnership speak of men and women who are connected and understand the heart of God. Again, this means a "shared vision" is at work. It all matters to God—every gift, assignment, and mantle are important!

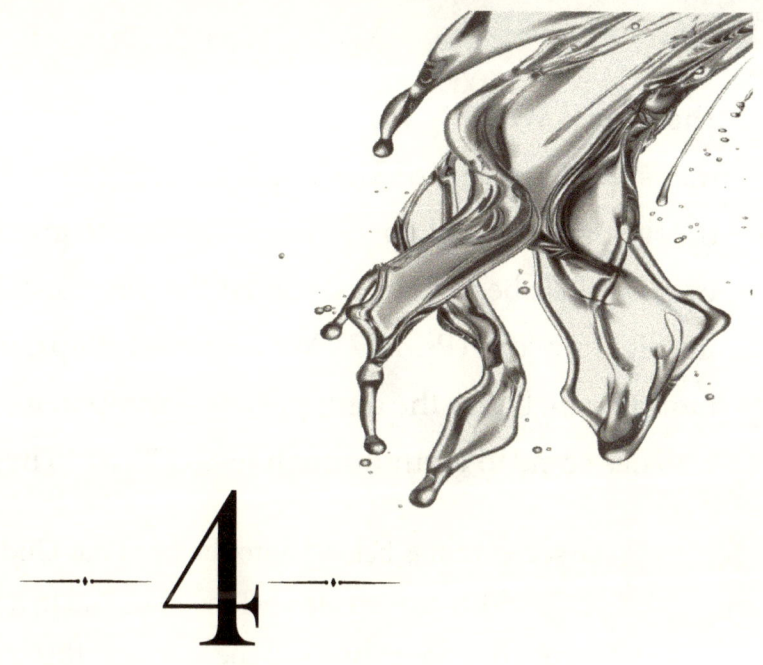

4

Kingdom Connectors

The Word, Worship & Warfare

The kingdom of God denotes a spiritual language that is needed for communication and comprehension as well as governmental administration that includes rules and mannerisms pertaining to alignment and order. The anointing flows out of this biblical configuration and causes deeper devotion and commitment to the things of God. It affects our responses in the natural and spiritual; it gives meaning and significance to all of our relationships.

> Thou wilt shew me the path of life: in thy presence is fullness of joy; at thy right hand there are pleasures for evermore.
>
> **Psalms 16:11**

The Word, Worship and Warfare connect us to the beauty and majesty of Jesus Christ! The Scriptures speak to us through examples. In Job 33:14-16, God opens the ears of men to give them instruction, even on their beds. David declared that the Lord instructed him in the night seasons (Ps. 16:7). We do not worship God as a weak, frail, mortal man, but as the omnipresent, omnipotent, omniscient God who has come to earth through Jesus Christ to live in us.

> The secret things belong unto the Lord our God; but those things which are revealed belong to us and to our children forever, that we may do all the words of this law.
>
> **DEUTERONOMY 29:29**

God wants us to know Him and be filled with His fullness. This signifies the capacity to understand and execute His will in every area of life (mentally, relationally, emotionally, financially, etc.). In short, it is a partnership that becomes our standard and way of life.

In this chapter, we will discuss three kingdom connectors. First, there is the Word, especially the preached word made applicable to the hearers. Second is worship, delighting oneself in the Lord. And finally, there is spiritual warfare—the invisible conflict all believers must face. We must be careful to maintain these connectors so that we can experience the fullness of what God has for us.

The Word

> In the beginning was the Word, and the Word was with God, and the Word was God. The same was in the beginning with God. …And the Word was made flesh, and dwelt among us…
>
> **John 1:1-3, 14**

The Word of God is Jesus Christ—and it is also the final, essential, and authoritative message of God to humanity as expressed in the pages of the Bible (1 John 1:1). He expressed this after His resurrection.

> And beginning at Moses and all the prophets, he expounded unto them in all the scriptures the things concerning himself. … Then opened he their understanding, that they might understand the scriptures.
>
> **Luke 24:27, 45**

A deep sense of reverence for and submission to the Word is important—it is our tool to equip us for our relationship to God and others. The Word was present from the beginning, and everything that God does He accomplishes through the power of His words.

After explaining all of this to the disciples, the command came to tarry in Jerusalem and wait for the arrival of the Holy Spirit and power for evangelization and confirming the Word with signs following (Acts 1:8). The preaching of the gospel is full of power—to save, to set free, and to deliver from the grip of sin and the devil (Acts 26:18).

It is an urgent message—we speak life even when it's inconvenient or uncomfortable. We are God's ambassadors (representatives). The apostles, prophets, evangelists, pastors and teachers equip the body for this work (Eph. 4:11). Power precedes presentation, and produces the desired result.

> But we will give ourselves continually to prayer, and to the ministry of the word.
>
> **ACTS 6:4**

Note the order here: a commitment to continual prayer first, and then the ministry of the Word. These two cannot be separated. Where the word flows in power, there was prayer to precede it—private or corporate.

Training for ministry is important, but ultimately, it is the anointing that destroys the yoke.

As we saw in the Tabernacle service, nothing was left to human thought. There is more to it than homiletic or hermeneutic skill. Training for ministry is important and necessary, but ultimately, it is the anointing that destroys the yoke (Isa. 10:27). Natural talent and professional skill are simply no substitute for the anointing. Prayer expresses dependence on the Lord to do what only He can do in a ministry, especially where deliverance is needed.

There is a lot of discussion about "relevance" today. But the word of the Lord can never be *irrelevant*. The changeless God speaks from eternity into our finite lives and situations, declaring the end from the beginning. Christ's ministers then become the stewards of God's mysteries.

> Let a man so account of us, as of the ministers of Christ, and stewards of the mysteries of God.
>
> 1 Corinthians 4:1

> The grass withereth, the flower fadeth: but the word of our God shall stand for ever.
>
> Isaiah 40:8

God establishes Himself in our lives through His Word. We must follow carefully where God leads and manage our internal conflicts through submission to His rule and lordship. Know when God is moving and always move at His pace. This will demonstrate your life's defining moments. It will serve as proof that you are in His perfect will and understand the capacity and capability of your God.

God's Word cuts to the deepest part of human nature, exposing hidden thoughts and motives. In a time of endless digital communication and social media, people are always speaking and sharing. But what are they really saying? In season and out, God's servants speak life and declare truth (2 Tim. 4:2).

> For the word of God is living and active and sharper than any two-edged sword, and piercing as far as the division of soul and spirit, of both joints and marrow, and able to judge the thoughts and intentions of the heart.
>
> **HEBREWS 4:12 NASB**

One example of what that looks like in a congregation that is connected and flowing:

> But if all prophesy, and there come in one that believeth not, or one unlearned, he is convinced of all, he is judged of all: And thus are the secrets of his heart made manifest; and so falling down on his face he will worship God, and report that God is in you of a truth.
>
> **1 CORINTHIANS 14:24-25**

Anyone can preach a sermon; but not everyone can bring a message. When the word is empowered by the anointing and blessed by God in its going forth, there will be results for the kingdom—breakthroughs, healings, salvation, and deliverance. The preached word releases: 1) conviction, 2) conversion, 3) connection, 4) conformity, 5) comfort, 6) clarity, and 7) change. The theologian Peter Forsyth wrote, "…it is authority that the world chiefly needs…an authoritative gospel in a humble personality."[1]

Worship

Worship is an act of reverence toward God expressed in public or in private. It includes praise, thanksgiving, adoration, blessing, and anything that exalts the name and person of Jesus Christ. It is essential to our life, not optional. It is prescribed by God for the good of the worshipper and for His glory; and those who draw near to minister to Him do so by divine commission and invitation.

In His conversation with the Samaritan woman, Jesus corrected a common misconception about worship. It is not limited to time and space alone or to a specific set of rituals alone. The visual aids of the Old Testament were tools pointing to the spiritual realities of Christ and the kingdom. Worship is a dynamic flow from our hearts to the heart of God!

> *Worship connects us to the heavenly worship service that is already in progress.*

In heaven, the worship is always taking place. We are told that the angels never cease their praises of the holiness and glory of God (Rev. 4:8-11). In fact, this is the main occupation of heaven! When we join in the corporate worship, or even tap into the presence of God in private, we are actually joining the service already in progress.

We must be aware of visible and invisible realities, natural and spiritual. There is more going on around you than what you can see. Faith is not sight! It believes God and perceives the invisible. When an army had surrounded the prophet Elisha and a fearful young man standing by, God pulled back the curtain and gave him a revelation of what was actually happening.

> And Elisha prayed, and said, LORD, I pray thee, open his eyes, that he may see. And the LORD opened the eyes of the young man; and he saw: and, behold, the mountain was full of horses and chariots of fire round about Elisha.
>
> 2 KINGS 6:17

> While we look not at the things which are seen, but at the things which are not seen: for the things which are seen are temporal; but the things which are not seen are eternal.
>
> 2 CORINTHIANS 4:18

He sends us the help when we need it most. May this inspire us to a fresh sense of the nearness of God's presence the next time we lift our hands with a "pure praise" and a "holy hallelujah."

> [Come] and, like living stones, be yourselves built [into] a spiritual house, for a holy (dedicated, consecrated) priesthood, to offer up [those] spiritual sacrifices [that are] acceptable and pleasing to God through Jesus Christ.
>
> 1 PETER 2:5 AMP

The church is called a kingdom of priests—called to offer acceptable sacrifices. This is both a privilege and a responsibility. The spiritual sacrifices we are called to offer include: our bodies as living sacrifices, our finances or resources, our faith, our intercession, and the sacrifice of praise—verbally and actively expressing ourselves to God![2]

There are many ways to show our love for God with all we have and are (Mark 12:30). There are those who display a kind of "it doesn't take all of that" attitude. Obviously, order is necessary and important, and I believe in order—but there's another level of release when an individual or congregation can go with the move of God in the present moment, even if it's not according to plan. Can you step out of your comfort zone if the Lord leads in a different direction?

Worship in truth depends on a clear understanding of who God is. The one true God is the God of Abraham, Isaac, and Jacob; the God who is revealed in Jesus Christ! When we worship, we are connecting with the living, resurrected King.

Jesus told the Samaritan woman that true worshippers will worship the Father in spirit and in truth, for they are the kind of worshippers the Father seeks (John 4:23). In other words, real worship will always be rooted in truth. But worship is offered to God in *spirit*. Clarke observes,

> A man worships God in spirit, when, under the influence of the Holy [Spirit], he brings all his affections, appetites, and desires to the throne of God; and he worships him in truth, when every purpose and passion of his heart, and

when every act of his religious worship, is guided and regulated by the word of God.³

To worship "in spirit," means out of our human spirits or innermost being. It is passion for God and His glory that He wants our hearts to be filled with—zeal with repentance, not lukewarmness (Rev. 3:16-19). This doesn't happen by just going through the motions—it takes sincerity and submission to the Holy Spirit. This is what moves you from blessing to presence.

> Let the word of Christ dwell in you richly in all wisdom; teaching and admonishing one another in psalms and hymns and spiritual songs, singing with grace in your hearts to the Lord.
>
> **COLOSSIANS 3:16**

Worship also affects the worshipper. It may be that there are changes we need to make for the next season, or to get back on track. We may need restoration or refreshing. It gives us an "aerial view" of circumstances and prompts us to adjust to the shifts or changes He wants us to make. In other words, "big" problems become smaller in His presence. Relationship and revelation are connected. Raise the volume of your worship and discover what will happen!

> After this I looked, and, behold, a door was opened in heaven: and the first voice which I heard was as it were of a trumpet talking with me; which said, Come up hither, and I will shew thee things which must be hereafter. And immediately I was in the spirit: and, behold, a throne was

set in heaven, and one sat on the throne. And he that sat was to look upon like a jasper and a sardine stone: and there was a rainbow round about the throne, in sight like unto an emerald.

REVELATION 4:1-3

The apostle John was one who worshipped and received information. A door in heaven was opened that led him to Christ on the throne. So we see that worship is never vague, but specific. You mature as you worship God for who He is, not just for what He does. Worship says God is worthy in spite of my circumstances. John was in exile at Patmos, but he knew how to get "in the Spirit on the Lord's Day!"

WARFARE

Spiritual warfare is the conflict by which we destroy strongholds and release deliverance. A stronghold literally means "a fortress" that is built up—it's a barrier representative of an idea or ideology that opposes the knowledge of God.[4] It is human reasoning manifested in the form of stubborn arguments. Spiritual warfare directly addresses thoughts, motives, and beliefs, as well as demonic forces.

> For though we walk in the flesh, we do not war after the flesh: (For the weapons of our warfare are not carnal, but mighty through God to the pulling down of strong holds;) Casting down imaginations, and every high thing that

> exalteth itself against the knowledge of God, and bringing into captivity every thought to the obedience of Christ;
>
> **2 Corinthians 10:3-5**

> Put on the whole armour of God, that ye may be able to stand against the wiles of the devil. For we wrestle not against flesh and blood, but against principalities, against powers, against the rulers of the darkness of this world, against spiritual wickedness in high places. Wherefore take unto you the whole armour of God, that ye may be able to withstand in the evil day, and having done all, to stand.
>
> **Ephesians 6:11-13**

Make no mistake, there is an unseen enemy! We don't fight with natural or physical weapons, but we have been given the Word of Jesus, the Name of Jesus, and the blood of Jesus. The armor, the gifts of the Spirit, the fruit of the Spirit, power in prayer, blessing through worship—the power of a godly life—these all enable us to stand before, during, and after the battle.

The renewing of spiritual warfare is an ongoing responsibility to those who understand that the forces of evil and demonic attacks are a constant threat to sustainable ministry. There are varying definitions of "strongholds," but we are coming against forceful, deeply-rooted rationales, opinions, ideas, or philosophies resistant to the knowledge of Jesus Christ. It is deceptive destruction.

The devil still uses "fiery darts" designed to kill and destroy.

Spiritual warriors respond successfully by taking these five steps: 1) recognizing what the strongholds are, 2) revealing their operation, 3) rebuking (binding and destroying) their control, 4) replacing lies with the truth of God's Word; and finally, 5) receiving the promised blessings.

> *Renewing spiritual warfare is an ongoing responsibility... demonic attacks are a constant threat to sustainable ministry.*

Spiritual warfare will happen to keep you from discovering your purpose, and when a prophetic word has been released over your life. Fight by the word of the Lord concerning you! He said to Joshua, "Have I not commanded you? Be strong and courageous" (Josh. 1:9). God has given us what we need to fulfill our assignments and purpose.

The victory in daily battles will not be handed to us—they require our attention and obedience (Ps. 98:1; 1 Cor. 15:57). Note: there is no armor given for the back! Even when things appear to be going well, stay watchful. God gives us authority and strategy to dismantle strongholds that impact every area of our life.

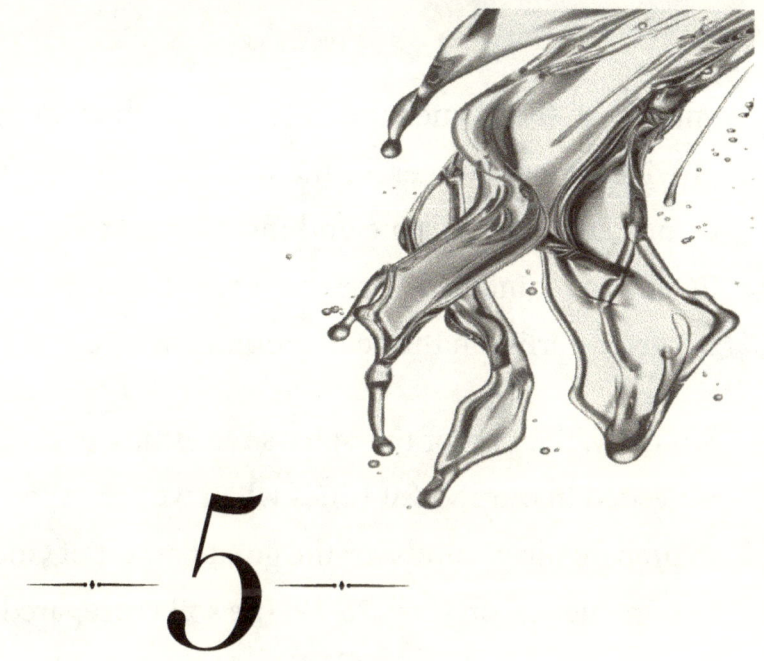

5

The Wheat

There are few symbols of the Word of God in Scripture as common as that of grain or bread. Although wheat is also called "corn" in Scripture, this does not refer to the maize grown in North America.[1] It most likely refers to either barley or wheat. Standing grain was covered with "chaff" which could be removed by rubbing the grain between one's hands, as the disciples did in Luke 6:1.

The agriculture of Bible times revolved around the seasons of seed time and harvest, which took place between November/December and April/May of each year. The health of the crops depended entirely on the former and latter rains, which did not last long, but provided enough water for them to thrive. These "wet seasons" also coincided with seedtime and ingathering.² The Feast of Weeks, or Pentecost, coincided with the wheat harvest—the barley harvest occurred earlier in the year, around Passover.

Similarly, the rain of the Spirit's refreshing to cultivate the ground is needed in our lives at times when we are called to sow, and also to prepare the grounds for the good harvest of God's will. He sends rain in due season (Lev. 26:4). The soil is prepared by plowshares—the plowing represents afflictions, especially those furrows laid on the backs of God's people by the attack of the enemy. It also speaks of repentance. Fallow ground must be broken up, so it can become good and useful, able to receive seed.³

> For thus saith the LORD to the men of Judah and Jerusalem,
> Break up your fallow ground, and sow not among thorns.
>
> **JEREMIAH 4:3**

> Sow to yourselves in righteousness, reap in mercy; break up your fallow ground: for it is time to seek the LORD, till he come and rain righteousness upon you.
>
> **HOSEA 10:12**

Wheat was the essential element for making bread and has been a staple of the world's diet in every generation. The imagery of wheat in Scripture serves as a metaphor as a nourisher and sustainer of life. The way grain was bruised, broken small, and reduced to meal fit to be made into bread is most interesting. The Christian life is filled with processes. In this day and time when many things are "instant," the wheat, wine, and oil remind us that preparation for usefulness takes time.

Wheat passes through several grinding processes. Once collected, the grain was brought to the threshing room floor, where it was crushed by oxen or iron wheels to remove the straw.[4] The resulting pile of grain was then tossed into the air with a fan so the chaff would be carried away by the wind, leaving the weightier grain on the ground.[5] This was called winnowing. To obtain a finer quality of wheat, this grain was then placed in a sieve to be sifted, or ground small between large millstones. Grinding at the mill was a daily activity for ancient families.

Keil and Delitzsch state, "The wheat was threshed upon open floors, or in places in the open field that were rolled hard for the purpose… Only poor people knocked out the little corn that they had gleaned with a stick."[6] Both Ruth and Gideon were found gleaning barley or wheat, and then beating it out to arrive at the true measure of what they had harvested (Ruth 2:17; Jdg. 6:11-13).

Wheat, which is good and profitable, is separated from the chaff (the wicked) and the tares, which represent hypocrites or false professors. God allows both types to grow together, but He will separate them in the end. He does this for the good of His children, so they won't be harmed in the uprooting process (Matt. 13:24-30). He is careful to protect what He's invested in us.

The Seed of the Word

Jesus often used illustrations from agriculture to teach spiritual lessons. From His parables we learn much about the kingdom of God and its operation, and the roles we play in His plan. For example, the Parable of the Sower in Matthew 13 tells us about the seed of the Word and its reception in the world. The field is a place of business, activity, and production. There is an expectation and hope of growth and abundance—but many internal factors can affect the ultimate outcome.

This parable gives great insight to the body of Christ everywhere, and the ministry of the local church as well. The seed of the Word is also called the word of the kingdom, and is the very means by which we are brought to the experience of new birth.

> Being born again, not of corruptible seed, but of incorruptible, by the word of God, which liveth and abideth for ever.
>
> **1 Peter 1:23**

If the seed is the gospel, then the sowers who go forth are those who carry the word with them, and preach it abroad. Success does not rest on the ability of the sower alone, but on the type of ground in which the seed lands—representing the four kinds of heart-attitudes present in the hearers.

> And when he sowed, some seeds fell by the way side, and the fowls came and devoured them up: Some fell upon stony places, where they had not much earth: and forthwith they sprung up, because they had no deepness of earth: And when the sun was up, they were scorched; and because they had no root, they withered away. And some fell among thorns; and the thorns sprung up, and choked them: But other fell into good ground, and brought forth fruit, some an hundredfold, some sixtyfold, some thirtyfold. Who hath ears to hear, let him hear.
>
> **Matthew 13:4-9**

In the first heart, the devil comes to devour the good word from the hearts of listeners. This person doesn't understand it—he fails to take the truth into his heart and let it take root.

In the second heart, there is attention paid to the word, and some belief in the truth, but not on the level that leads to repentance and regeneration. There are those who sit in church, sometimes for years, and yet never come to genuine faith—and when persecution or hardship comes, they stumble or are offended.[7]

In the third heart, the good word is literally choked and overrun by the anxieties of this life, worldliness, and the "deceitfulness of riches," which pretend to offer security and blessing, but fall short of spiritual life. This stifling of the word is where the love of money leads (1 Tim. 6:7-11). There's nothing wrong with you having money or things—but something *is* wrong if they have you!

The fourth heart is the "good ground" where the truth is received and is fruitful. Genuine believers will manifest a desire to bear fruit. This group of hearers deliberately and willingly embraces truth and fulfills the purpose of the sower. The level of fruitfulness varies based on "characters and capacities and gifts."[8]

> *Don't just hear with your natural ear. Hear with understanding. Hear with faith.*

Jesus is saying, don't just hear with your natural ear—hear with understanding. Hear with faith. True hearing leads to obedience. One can believe what they do not fully understand. But it's the truth you understand that really makes you free.

Nourishment & Sustenance

Psalm 81:15 speaks of "the finest of the wheat." This is not just abundance but denotes how effective the wheat is. Another example of wheat as the nourisher or sustainer appears in the temptation of Jesus found in Luke 4:1-13. With each temptation, Jesus used the Word as a sword—a weapon against the enemy—to sustain Himself.

When tempted with food, His response was "man shall not live by bread alone" (v. 4). After offering Jesus all the kingdoms of the world, again the devil was wounded with the truth of the Word: "It is written, thou shalt worship the Lord thy God and Him only shalt thou serve" (v. 8). In a final attempt, the devil tempts Jesus to prove His deity. The Word used was "thou shalt not tempt the Lord thy God" (v. 12). Now here is the evidence of how powerful that response was: the devil left Jesus and fled the scene! It is absolutely necessary that Christians are equipped with the power of the Word for nourishment and sustenance.

The Word sustains us daily (Pr. 15:23). There is a blessing for those who search the Word with diligence. The example of the Bereans and Paul's word to Timothy both demonstrate this.

> These were more noble than those in Thessalonica, in that they received the word with all readiness of mind, and searched the scriptures daily, whether those things were so.
>
> **ACTS 17:11**

> Study to shew thyself approved unto God, a workman that needeth not to be ashamed, rightly dividing the word of truth.
>
> **2 TIMOTHY 2:15**

There are those who "fit" the word into their schedules. It becomes a matter of convenience or leisure. Bible study or Christian education is necessary for spiritual growth. Imagine eating a meal only once a week on Sundays! It takes the incense of prayer and worship and the bread of the Word to produce mature sons and daughters. When you hear a message, what do you "glean?" In other words, how much is retained, applied, and fruitful in your life?

The Word renews our minds and transforms our thinking (Rom. 12:2). Sadly, some are unwilling to change their ideas or opinions, and remain stuck. Change comes to the teachable spirit who does not mind being confronted with truth. But it's not just the word we "know," but what's hidden in our heart that keeps guards against sin (Ps. 119:11).

> Therefore whosoever heareth these sayings of mine, and doeth them, I will liken him unto a wise man, which built his house upon a rock…
>
> MATTHEW 7:24-25

> Therefore we ought to give the more earnest heed to the things which we have heard, lest at any time we should let them slip.
>
> HEBREWS 2:1

> But be ye doers of the word, and not hearers only, deceiving your own selves.
>
> JAMES 1:22-25

A Word of Encouragement

Genesis 28 records a "wrestling match" with the Angel of the Lord in which Jacob wins by faith. The narrative tells us that Jacob wanted to know the name of the angel out of sheer desperation. I believe this represented at least in part the core of his lifelong desire for the blessing of God. He was able to grasp and hold on to the One true giver of life. It seems as if his faith was both drawn and driven. It was drawn because He recognized that God was releasing another level of manifestation. It was driven by the emptiness, and yes, the guilt of his past.

Jacob claimed the promise (God's words). The entire event ends with the Lord Himself pronouncing Jacob a winner. His name was instantly changed from a word denoting a "trickster" to one who now had prevailing power with God. He struggled and wept for favor and won. How did he accomplish this? It wasn't that he had pinned his opponent down. No, he was helpless and realized his power was gone. Jacob received the blessing in the dawning light.

> *Day will eventually break, and when it does, you will know that you have been with God.*

Perhaps, dear reader, your struggle seems long and is just overwhelming, but the day will break. And when it does, you will know that you have been with God! May a new glory inspire and enrich your life. May it energize your fight to win and bring forth a deeper praise to God.

THE BREAD OF GOD

The thought of bread as nourishment is also seen in manna, the food God provided for the Israelites in the wilderness. Although it was not made of wheat, Jesus explained that this bread really typified Himself as the Bread of Life.

> Then Jesus said unto them, Verily, verily, I say unto you, Moses gave you not that bread from heaven; but my Father giveth you the true bread from heaven. For the bread of God is he which cometh down from heaven, and giveth life unto the world.
>
> **John 6:32-33**

Jesus was saying that to receive Him was so much more than natural nourishment. To partake of Him was to receive everlasting life—sustenance for the soul. He had come from heaven to provide life to the world, if only they would receive it.

Wheat appears in the form of bread again in the symbols of the Lord's table. It represents the physical body of Jesus Christ, broken for us in physical suffering (Luke 22:19). Jesus compared Himself to a grain of wheat falling into the ground, dying alone. It had to happen that way, so it could produce the abundance of harvest (John 12:24). Bread also represents all believers, unified and sharing in the common blessing (1 Cor. 10:16-17). It is a time to remember, to renew faith, and to announce the Lord's death until His return.

Finally, I suggest to you that the "digestion" of spiritual truth denotes prevention against the discouragements, doubts, and distractions that come our way in life. The word reveals God in many ways…one could say it is His testimony! When we speak of our revelation of Him through the Word, we touch the reality of who God is to us. Just as the prophets of old knew God as J<small>EHOVAH</small>-J<small>IREH</small> or J<small>EHOVAH</small>-N<small>ISSI</small>, when we touch Him, we now move beyond mere human comprehension, we touch God Himself.

6

The Wine

We have discussed Christ our Intercessor; the power of prayer; moving from blessing to presence; and the three kingdom connectors. We then discovered that wheat represents what the Word of God is to us: our nourishment and sustenance. That brings us now to the wine, and what its symbolism means for our spiritual life.

The vintage came to fruition in September, after the barley and wheat harvests, but in time for the Feast of Ingathering at the end of the year. The Israelites could not eat the fruit during the first three years of planting. In the fourth year all fruit was dedicated to the Lord (Deut. 18:4). The following year, it could be eaten freely (Lev. 19:23-25).

Winepresses were common in the Bible lands. They were made up of two vats, a higher and a lower, and usually hewn out of stone. The grapes were placed in the upper vat, then a number of men would "tread" or step on them to release the juice.[1] The juice then ran down a narrow drain in to the second vat, where it was collected in various vessels.[2]

It is powerful that after all the work of growing the grapes, they had to be "crushed" before they could produce anything! The process is painful, but the reward is sweet. Again, this teaches us that in order for God to bring out the good He has placed within you, there must be a crushing or a bruising in your life (Pr. 20:30). Interesting, the purest juice was released by the grapes of its own accord, through natural pressure, before the treading began. These first drops of wine were referred to by a Hebrew word meaning "tears" (Ex. 22:29). The firstfruits were always dedicated to God.

Wine was used in many ancient rituals of worship, but again, God uses these tangible items to illuminate spiritual realities. Jacob was the first to anoint the pillar of stone with oil and wine at Bethel, which represents the house of God. Under the Law, drink offerings (probably unfermented wine) accompanied meal offerings and other sacrifices on the altar of burnt offering. The winepress, like the winnowing fan in our discussion of wheat, is also associated with God's judgment or wrath (Rev. 14:10).

NOT SURPRISED

God is never surprised by our circumstances. Surprise really means you didn't know. Omniscience knows all possible outcomes of every situation in advance. He promises to take this endless maze of possibilities and work them for good. If you love God, it's working for your good. If you are called, it's working for your good!

> And we know that all things work together for good to them that love God, to them who are the called according to his purpose.
>
> **ROMANS 8:28**

God created Adam and Eve with a purpose. He prepared a place for them, gave them life, and pronounced the blessing of "good" over everything. Adam only had to worship, subdue the earth, multiply, and rule over animal life. God was not surprised by Adam's failure. But disobedience and sin have hurt our relationship with God. Sin distorts perception and threatens destiny. It falls short and misses the mark. Adam missed his "appointment" with God…and God sought him out to call him to account.

God begins by asking questions. Note that God is not asking because He needs to know anything, but so they will see their own condition. He asked Adam, "Where are you?" (Gen. 3:9). And to Eve, "What have you done?" (Gen. 3:13). To Cain it was, "Where is your brother?"

(Gen. 4:9). And to Elijah, He asked, "What are you doing here?" (1 Ki. 19:9). In the New Testament, the pattern continues. He asked Saul of Tarsus (at his conversion), "Why are you persecuting me?" And to Peter, "Do you love me more than these?" There are countless examples. In every situation, the answer led to a revelation of guilt or a reproof regarding the true state of that person's heart.

> The gospel gives us everything: cleansing through the blood, a new spiritual nature, and the power to live a holy life.

This reminds us of the real purpose of the Law—which is to reveal sin. It shows the strict justice of God and proves that all are sinners by nature and practice (Rom. 3:20-23). But the gospel gives us everything: cleansing through the blood, a new spiritual nature, and the power to live a holy life (Rom. 3:24-26). Spiritually, we are called to connect with God, investing ourselves in good works that bring glory to Him (Matt. 5:16).

Again, God was not surprised by Israel's failure, but made provision for it. When He gave the Law, He also provided the sacrificial system so that worshippers could approach through types and symbols pointing to the shed blood of Jesus Christ. Why blood? It is because life is in the blood, and without the shedding of blood there is no remission of sin (Heb. 9:22).

SEEKERS REWARD

> But without faith it is impossible to please him: for he that cometh to God must believe that he is, and that he is a rewarder of them that diligently seek him.
>
> **HEBREWS 11:6**

People ask, "How can I please God?" A simple answer is, "by believing Him." This means accepting His existence and the nature of who He is, but also that those who diligently seek Him will find their commitment and devotion rewarded.

God had once called Israel His "noble vine," and spoke of a day when they would walk in heartfelt covenant with the Lord, enjoying an abundance of earthly blessing (Isa. 61:9; Jer. 2:21). But they rebelled, blasphemed, and even burned incense to other gods (Isa. 65:1-7). He spread out His hands, welcoming them—inviting them to come toward His presence and receive blessing—but they would not come (v. 2). Their self-righteousness arose in His nose like a smoke that stung the eyes and was a source of irritation, so opposite of the fragrance once offered by the holy incense (v. 5).

> And there is none that calleth upon thy name, that stirreth up himself to take hold of thee: for thou hast hid thy face from us, and hast consumed us, because of our iniquities.
>
> **ISAIAH 64:7**

The prophet Isaiah interceded for them, hoping that God would intervene and not punish them as they deserved. The Lord answered that there would still be judgment, but there was good news for those who sought after God.

> Thus saith the LORD, As the new wine is found in the cluster, and one saith, Destroy it not; for a blessing is in it: so will I do for my servants' sakes, that I may not destroy them all. And I will bring forth a seed out of Jacob, and out of Judah an inheritor of my mountains: and mine elect shall inherit it, and my servants shall dwell there. And Sharon shall be a fold of flocks, and the valley of Achor a place for the herds to lie down in, for my people that have sought me.
>
> **Isaiah 65:8-10**

For the righteous among them, there was hope. Just as a farmer would not destroy all of the grapes if some were still good, so He would bring forth and bless His elect servants, and not destroy them all. God's nature is to save and to spare. The good wine (juice) represents the anointing and the blessing that was in His servants.

God was saying to the faithful remnant that He would still use them, bless them, and settle them. The servants are forever linked with Jacob, the one who moved from blessing to presence by wrestling in prayer until the breaking of day. They are also connected to Judah, which speaks of praise and worship. Once again, the combination of prayer, praise, and worship appear together.

The Lord promises that those who seek Him will be rewarded. Sharon and Achor illustrate this. Sharon was a beautiful and fruitful place near the Mediterranean coast, offering watering or replenishment, and fertile ground for planting. Though it had become like a wilderness, God promises to restore the land to fullness so that it will be a fold of flocks for His people.[3] God is a restorer. He is able to turn things around, so that your latter is greater than the former.

The Valley of Achor (or, "trouble") was located near Jericho and had become known for the sin and stoning of Achan in the days of Joshua (Josh. 7:24). Joy would characterize a place once synonymous with "causing affliction."[4] God turns a place of trouble and punishment for His people into a door of hope! (Hos. 2:15). Do you need to recover from some "trouble" in your life? Don't stop seeking Him, no matter what is happening around you. He is a rewarder!

> Jesus sanctifies our joys and our sorrows for His purpose and glory.

The initial miracle performed by Christ took place at the wedding at Cana, when He turned water into wine (John 2:1-11). When informed that the hosts had no more left, Mary speaks to Jesus, who responded that the situation had nothing to do with either of them (John 2:4). He instructed the servants to fill the waterpots and dip out the water (now turned into wine) and present it to the host. This miracle speaks of the level of obedience by the servants and is a miraculous display of Christ's glory as He portrays the joy of life. Indeed, Jesus Christ sanctifies our joys and our sorrows for His purpose and glory!

The Precious Blood

While wine represents natural joy and blessing, most prominently, it directs us to the blood of Jesus Christ. This is the remedy for the breach caused by sin in the Fall. He provided for the first man and woman a covering that pointed to Christ. We read:

> Unto Adam also and to his wife did the LORD God make coats of skins, and clothed them.
>
> **Genesis 3:21**

There we see the covering provided at the expense of another. The life of blessing does not come without cost! It is a price that cannot be compared to money.

> Forasmuch as ye know that ye were not redeemed with corruptible things, as silver and gold…But with the precious blood of Christ, as of a lamb without blemish and without spot:
>
> **1 Peter 1:18-19**

And the fruit of the vine, which is pressed to release its sweet juice, gives us illumination regarding the sweetness of the gospel of Jesus Christ. The blood is an active cleansing agent when applied to the sinning soul. No wonder Jesus commanded us to observe communion with the wine (grape juice) as an emblem of His sacrificial outpouring. Matthew Henry gives this insight:

> The blood of Christ is signified and represented by the wine. He gave thanks, to teach us to look to God in every part of the ordinance. This cup he gave to the disciples with a command, Drink…all of it. The pardon of sin is that great blessing which is, in the Lord's supper, conferred on all true believers; it is the foundation of all other blessings.[5]

The apostle Paul refers to "the cup of blessing" which we share in common (1 Cor. 10:16). Through the blood, we experience redemption, forgiveness of sins, the purging of the conscience from dead works, and protection from the judgment of God (Col. 1:14; Rev. 1:5). It is the seal of the New Covenant—by which we know we are redeemed from the curse of the Law. Thank God for the blood!

> How much more shall the blood of Christ, who through the eternal Spirit offered himself without spot to God, purge your conscience from dead works to serve the living God?
>
> **HEBREWS 9:14**

The Christian observance of communion is biblically connected to the Jewish feast of Passover. Again, Jehovah of the Old Testament means God in covenant relationship. He chose Israel to teach all nations the concept of monotheism (One God) and to bring Messiah (Jesus Christ) to the world. When Pharaoh refused to release the

Israelites from Egyptian bondage, the Lord poured out plague after plague of judgment, ending in death (Ex. 11:5).

God's purpose in redemption was finalized by the sacrificial lamb and the blood applied on the tops and sides of the door frames of every home. This demonstrated God's mercy and perfect provision—the substitution of a life for a life. Jesus is our "pass-over lamb," sacrificing His life for our redemption. Again, the communion table with its elements of bread and wine, typify His body and blood by faith. What a blessing that true believers have access and fellowship with Christ as we remember His death and suffering.

The reading of Scriptures and singing of what early Christians called the "blood or redemption song" brings praise to our redeemer, Jesus Christ. For example, consider the words of the classic hymn, popularly known as "At the Cross":

> Alas! and did my Savior bleed
> And did my Sovereign die?
> Would He devote that sacred head
> For such a worm as I?
>
> **Refrain:**
> *At the cross, at the cross where I first saw the light,*
> *And the burden of my heart rolled away,*
> *It was there by faith I received my sight,*
> *And now I am happy all the day!*[6]

Abide in the Vine

The study of the Word draws us into His presence. It is vital that believers are taught sound bible doctrine. This means the life, death burial and resurrection of Jesus Christ. When the truth of the gospel of Jesus Christ is taught, believed, and practiced, it determines our behavior and the course of our destiny in God.

In ancient times, wine was a necessity because of the scarcity of water and became an image of sustenance and life. In this relationship, wheat (the Word) and oil (the anointing and presence of God) denotes covenant and the blessings promised by God to the obedient and those who are faithful to the truth of the gospel.

Jesus gives us an extended teaching on the fruit of the vine in John 15. He shows us the secret to experiencing this blessing: abiding in Him. It is by resting and receiving, living and walking in the flow of His precious anointing and in the new reality which cleansing from sin gives us that we learn to abide.

As you allow Him to bring the pruning and purging work of correction into your life, fruit, more fruit, and much fruit will come in its successive seasons. Then you will reach a place of maturity in God that understands the process and is fully submitted to its phases and experiences.

> Now ye are clean through the word which I have spoken unto you. Abide in me, and I in you. As the branch cannot

bear fruit of itself, except it abide in the vine; no more can ye, except ye abide in me. I am the vine, ye are the branches: He that abideth in me, and I in him, the same bringeth forth much fruit: for without me ye can do nothing.

JOHN 15:3-5

The Word of God is the pruning knife we are called to submit to. Stay clean through the Word (John 15:3; Eph. 5:26). Pray with expectation that He will restore, refresh, and renew your life. Rejoice in Christ's redemption and keep being filled with the Spirit (Eph. 5:18). No matter what it looks like or what "trouble" you are facing, it's not over. There's a blessing in it, and He is still working for your good. Hallelujah!

Consecration of Aaron and His Sons, illustration from the 1890 Holman Bible, 1890.

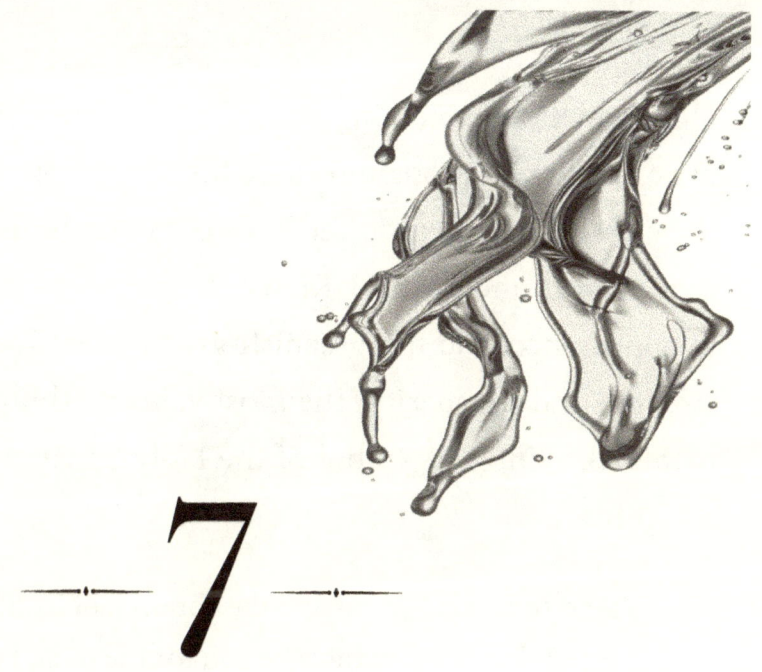

7

THE OIL

Oil has been a valuable commodity in many cultures, ancient and modern. In addition to being used in food and preparations for the dead, it also has cosmetic, medicinal, and spiritual significance. When God gave Moses instructions to prepare a sanctuary, He included instructions to prepare two special mixtures for regular use—the holy incense and the anointing oil. It brings us into a discussion of the sanctification processes of life and our position as sons and daughters in the kingdom of God.

Olives grew in groves and were very common in biblical times in

Judea and the surrounding areas. They become ripe around August or September. King Solomon used the wood of the olive tree to form the massive cherubim in the Holy of Holies in the temple, as well as the doors and posts (1 Ki. 6:23). The tree is twisty and knotty in appearance, and has greenish-gray leaves. The olive speaks of strength and prosperity. The most valuable thing about the olive is the oil.[1] Oil is a symbol of the Holy Spirit as it relates to the anointing.

> And thou shalt command the children of Israel, that they bring thee pure oil olive beaten for the light, to cause the lamp to burn always.
>
> **EXODUS 27:20**

Olive oil served two purposes in the Mosaic tabernacle. It was used as an ingredient in a special mixture, but it was also used in its pure form to light the lamp of the inner sanctuary. The Golden Candlestick was to remain lit at all times, and each morning and evening, the priests ensured that fresh oil was added to the seven-branched candlestick. We can say, in His light we see light (Ps. 36:9). Our life and service is performed in the light of truth.

> But if we walk in the light, as he is in the light, we have fellowship one with another, and the blood of Jesus Christ his Son cleanseth us from all sin.
>
> **1 JOHN 1:7**

Just as with the wine, the first drops of the oil were the purest, and just a small break in the fruit would release it. But the pure oil was squeezed out in the press, it was "beaten" with a mortar and pestle. This was called the "mother drop" of oil.² In the press, we see that outside "pressure" is applied to release its inner richness.

> When one considers the oil of God, is motivates us to think and experience the hands of the anointer!

When one considers the oil of God, is motivates us to think and experience the hands of the Anointer! This penetrating "hands-on" concept is the anointing of our lives. Being filled with the Spirit is also being formed by the Spirit. "I shall be anointed with fresh oil" (Ps 92:10).

Similar to the incense, the oil was not to be used casually. The elements retrieved by the priests where "principal spices." The Tabernacle, its vessels, and the altar, were consecrated. Aaron and his sons were also consecrated to minister as priests. Further, it was commanded to be holy anointing oil throughout Israel's generations. Any improper use would cause one to be cut off from the community. Again, the Old Testament example serves as a sobering reminder in our day and time to take great care in how we make use of the precious oil of God!

Prayer, Bible study, and submission to Christ are all a part of sanctification. If the oil of God is a flow of His life through us, then we can increase or decrease that expression either through diligence or negligence.

Further, the Holy Spirit is with and in us, and that means there are gifts and graces that come with evidence and manifestation. There should be a clear manifestation of the gifts, graces, and fruit (love, joy, peace, etc). There is a time when one needs to be anointed with fresh oil, and renew one's understanding of the elements of God's holy anointing.

> But my horn shalt thou exalt like the horn of an unicorn:
> I shall be anointed with fresh oil.
>
> **PSALMS 92:10**

PRESENCE, NOT POSITION

Although the anointing brings gifts, gifts do not supersede order. God uses a process of discipline within the context of spiritual sonship to establish and maintain order. David was anointed king as a teenager, but he was not ready to sit on the throne that day. He was chosen by God's "law of selection," and was gifted as well—but he had to be submitted, trained, and endure many trials and afflictions before he was mature enough to reign and rule (1 Sam. 18:5).

This is a powerful lesson for believers today. Position does not make one anointed. The presence of God meant everything to David—he preferred it above all else. Elisha understood this, and walked as a servant to Elijah until he was taken up. Jesus knew His purpose and calling, but remained subject to His parents as His level of (earthly) maturity demanded—until the time He was publicly announced at His baptism (Luke 2:46-52; 3:22). Jesus spent three years investing in the lives of His disciples, but they still couldn't go forth in fullness without the baptism of the Holy Spirit. They endured hardship, faced fears, experienced personal failures, and were scattered as God worked with them and used them.

The New Testament provides a good example: Paul trained Timothy, whom he called his "son in the faith." Timothy sat at his feet and learned with a teachable spirit from his spiritual father. The oil of God always flows from the head down (see also Num. 11:25). Eventually, Timothy had come to the point where he needed to overcome timidity and step out into the fullness of his own ministry.

> …It is like the precious ointment upon the head, that ran down upon the beard, even Aaron's beard: that went down to the skirts of his garments;
>
> **PSALMS 133:1-2**

> This charge I commit unto thee, son Timothy, according to the prophecies which went before on thee, that thou by them mightest war a good warfare;
>
> **1 TIMOTHY 1:18**

> Neglect not the gift that is in thee, which was given thee by prophecy, with the laying on of the hands of the presbytery.
>
> 1 TIMOTHY 4:14

THE MIXING OF THE OILS

The concept for this book was originally birthed out of a desire to understand more about the anointing and its use after having read the passage in Exodus 30. After teaching it during a mid-week Bible study, I realized God wanted to show me more. My desire to understand more caused me to research and study, always depending on the Holy Spirit to bring clarity to the Word of God relative to the Art of the Apothecary.

After finding a Christian company that sold the elements, the road to a service of demonstration was well underway. The leadership quickly grasps the concept and has developed it in such a way, that people began asking for oil on a regular basis. We have received praise reports of healing and deliverance here in the U.S. and even in places outside the country where testimonies continue to be reported.

Today, Christ Church International hosts "The Art of the Apothecary: the Mixing of the Oils" annually. On this highly-anticipated and prophetic occasion, various preachers speak on the ingredients of the holy anointing oil and their spiritual significance and application to our lives today.

Its Composition

> Moreover the LORD spake unto Moses, saying, Take thou also unto thee principal spices, of pure myrrh five hundred shekels, and of sweet cinnamon half so much, even two hundred and fifty shekels, and of sweet calamus two hundred and fifty shekels, And of cassia five hundred shekels, after the shekel of the sanctuary, and of oil olive an hin: And thou shalt make it an oil of holy ointment, an ointment compound after the art of the apothecary: it shall be an holy anointing oil.
>
> Exodus 30:22-25)

The anointing oil was comprised of five ingredients. Pure olive oil was the base, and myrrh, cinnamon, cassia, and calamus were added to it. Just as the incense, each ingredient had to be gathered and prepared separately before it could reach a usable state. Each element will give us some insight into the nature of the true anointing.

> *God can "grace" you in such a way that you can live victoriously in the midst of imperfect people.*

The number five is symbolic of God's grace to man and the responsibility of man. Grace is undeserved favor. It is also capability. Grace gives you integrity in the face of a challenging or competitive situations. When tempted to do whatever it takes to win, grace will move you to let the faithfulness of Word settle the issue. When you wrestle with mixed feelings or sketchy information, grace causes you to deal with known principles of godliness. At times when you feel weak, grace makes you rely on God more than your physical strength. God can "grace" you in such a way that you can live victoriously in the midst of imperfect people (1 Cor. 1:25, 27).

Myrrh

Myrrh is a gum-oil resin that gets its name from the Arabic word *murr*, which means "bitterness." When the bark is cut, it releases a yellowish resin which turns to a reddish-brown color in the form of teardrops. The purest form of myrrh flows spontaneously from the bark. Because of it's free flowing sap, it is also called "Myrrh of Freedom."[3] It was used in purification rituals, embalming, as a preservative, and when mixed with other elements, can be an anesthetic.

"The Bitter Truth"

In 2012, Elder LaSonya Thomas released a message at the oil mixing service titled, "The Bitter Truth," which is presented here, in part, for your edification:

In this study, we will focus on myrrh as it was used when presented to Jesus by the magi, highlighting its purpose in connection with the anointing oil, and relating it to our lives.

> And when they were come into the house, they saw the young child with Mary his mother, and fell down, and worshipped him: and when they had opened their treasures, they presented unto him gifts; gold, and frankincense, and myrrh.
>
> **MATTHEW 2:11**

The wise men's gifts were strategically chosen. The gold represented the Son's salvation; the frankincense represented the Son's holiness; and myrrh represented the Son's suffering. What we learn from this is that we are supposed to endure the bitter in order to be exposed to the truth, and truth will cause us to come out better.

Myrrh not only represents what is bitter, but it symbolizes suffering, trial, tribulation, and affliction. Myrrh adds depth to the incense and other perfume blends. Depth correlates to intensity, strength, and power. Even though he was a Son, He went through suffering and persecution from His birth to His death. Because of Jesus's obedience in His bitter season, we are now heirs to this powerful anointing—as long as we are obedient as well.

> Who in the days of his flesh, when he had offered up prayers and supplications with strong crying and tears unto him that was able to save him from death, and was heard in that he feared; Though he were a Son, yet learned he obedience by the things which he suffered; And being made perfect, he became the author of eternal salvation unto all them that obey him.
>
> **HEBREWS 5:7-9**

The myrrh is an important ingredient in our anointing as God's sons and daughters. So ask yourself: should we try to avoid our myrrh seasons? Or are we supposed to go through the myrrh season to have a complete balance in our anointing? The myrrh gives us depth, power, and strength. That is why we cannot seek to avoid the process that God has prepared for us. We need a balance of all the spices in this anointing oil from God in order for Him to have free course in us.

> Why do we want to avoid the myrrh in our lives? It's because the myrrh season is not attractive to us.

Why do we want to avoid the myrrh in our lives? It's because the myrrh season is not attractive to us. It makes our lives seem confused, and this confusion is illustrated by the knots and twists that form the bark of the myrrh tree. It may seem like hardest season of our lives because at that point we are being exposed to the truth. The bitter element is needed in this anointing because it is a major part of a Christian's development. The bitter will either break you or make you stronger. The bitter will not only show you who you are, it will show you who is for you and who is against you. The bitter will push you to seek after more of the truth.

We will all go through bitter seasons in life, especially if we are chasing after the truth. In order for us to operate and flow in our anointing, we have to allow all these oils to be mixed together and work. We cannot just receive the sweet spices or promises from God, but then forget the truth that dwells within us when myrrh comes along. The truth is what gives us power to overcome myrrh-like situations. Jesus did not have the option of choosing His myrrh season, and neither do we.

The bitter truth led Jesus to His destiny, made Jesus able to cast out demons, and allowed Jesus to call the dead back to life. This bitter truth made Jesus love so much that He died for our sins. We have to go through the bitter to receive illumination from the truth in order for us to come out better!

People need to smell the fragrance of this bitter truth because it is an aroma that cannot be duplicated. This is your own personal suffering (anointing scent), and during this season of bitter truth we will gain a greater understanding God's plan. The fragrance will become a walking, talking, testimonial of truth within us.

> Who now rejoice in my sufferings for you, and fill up that which is behind of the afflictions of Christ in my flesh for his body's sake, which is the church:
>
> **COLOSSIANS 1:24**

It says to REJOICE NOW in these trials, or myrrh times. The now represents present circumstances. So rejoice, which is in the active voice, means to rejoice now, during the suffering. We rejoice in the moment—not after it is over.

In spite of whatever is lacking (not complete) in your life, rejoice. Paul made a choice to rejoice in the midst of his sufferings for Christ. There should be a change in your countenance … a new scent, a new odor, a new aroma, and a new you. This mixture is an original and was specifically prepared with a specific combination of oils (especially the myrrh). Therefore, this truth cannot be imitated, faked, or copied. If you find that you can imitate someone else's anointing, then is that really the anointing you want?

> *If you find that you can imitate someone else's anointing, is that really the anointing you want?*

As stated earlier, in order for someone to gather myrrh from the plant, a person had to cut into the bark and allow the sap to ooze out. It is time for us to do some cutting in our lives in order to get to the truth.

The good news is that God does not discard the sap that has been cut out of our lives; God has a purpose for everything that we have gone through or will be going through. He allows us to identify the bitter in someone else who may be a babe in Christ—and it is our responsibility to guide and restore that person to the truth. We can do this because we have both the bitter truth and a balance of the anointed oils working in us.

> Howbeit when he, the Spirit of truth, is come, he will guide you into all truth: for he shall not speak of himself; but whatsoever he shall hear, that shall he speak: and he will shew you things to come.
>
> **JOHN 16:13**

What is the truth? Truth can protect you (Ps. 40:11). Truth can guide you (Ps. 43:4). Truth has the power to set you free from bondage of sin (John 8:31). Truth will allow you to worship Him freely (John 4:24). God said that He is near to those who call on Him in truth (Ps. 145:18). Before this myrrh season, we distorted truth (due to self-seeking) and led people astray—but after the myrrh season, we have been exposed to the truth and will come out better!

We'll know we are better when we stop worrying about people from the past, because we will understand better why they didn't make it to our future. The better is when we are able to see past someone's exterior and recognize that he or she is anointed. The better is when God takes something from our hands and we let it go, understanding that it's not a punishment, but that He wants our hands free to hold something greater. The will of God will never take you where the grace of God will not protect you!

The better will make you love people and not know why; push people into their destiny without any insecurity on your part; and allow you to raise up the next generation in proper order. The better will make you stop focusing on what you should have done or could have been, and make you laugh when you should be crying.

Now I pray that we will understand the importance of all the elements of the oil, no longer avoiding the myrrh. We can choose to "rejoice now" in our myrrh season, because now we understand the "bitter truth" (Thomas 2012).**

Cinnamon

Cinnamon is a sweet, fragrant spice that grows in the region of Sri Lanka and other places. The Hebrew word, *qinnâmôn*, denotes stability or firmness.[4] Cinnamon is taken from the inner bark, but to get to it, the outer bark must go through a process of scraping, and sometimes pounding.

Very often, God will put us in situations that "scrape" us. The bark speaks to us of the resolve and faith needed to withstand the difficulties and challenges that come against us. Instead of giving up, we will hold on.

> And not only so, but we glory in tribulations also: knowing that tribulation worketh patience; And patience, experience; and experience, hope: And hope maketh not ashamed; because the love of God is shed abroad in our hearts by the Holy Ghost which is given unto us.
>
> **Romans 5:3-5**

Cinnamon is working in your life when you can glory in tribulations. You will mature to the point that it's worth it for the fruit of the process: patience, experience, and hope. In spite of what you are going through, the sweetness of the love of God will fill and sustain you.

> Who shall separate us from the love of Christ? shall tribulation, or distress, or persecution, or famine, or nakedness, or peril, or sword? As it is written, For thy sake we are killed all the day long; we are accounted as sheep for the slaughter. Nay, in all these things we are more than conquerors through him that loved us. For I am persuaded, that neither death, nor life, nor angels, nor principalities, nor powers, nor things present, nor things to come, Nor height, nor depth, nor any other creature, shall be able to separate us from the love of God, which is in Christ Jesus our Lord.
>
> **ROMANS 8:35-39**

Paul suggests that he had been dealing with difficult things or people for some time. He had suffered significantly, and faced grueling times in ministry. He was convinced, and could not be swayed by public opinion, even in the midst of dangerous circumstances. He proved resolute in his decision to trust in God, knowing that none of the difficulties were enough to separate him from the love of God. This is a powerful truth! We must know that God's love never fails, and no power can disconnect us from that life-changing, paternal reality.

Calamus

The next ingredient mentioned is *calamus*, which grows mainly among marsh grass (wetlands). It was also called a sweet cane, reed, rope, or bulrush—valued for its aromatic and medicinal properties. It was the scraping of the root. It grew as a swamp plant among other twigs and stalks. The term "a reed shaken by the wind," as Jesus used it, denoted one who was easily moved, unsteady, not necessarily stable enough to deal with opposition.[5] John was the opposite of this. More commonly, it is said to represent weakness, frailty, and one's sense of brokenness under the weight of calamity or a sense of their own sinfulness.[6]

> He shall not cry, nor lift up, nor cause his voice to be heard in the street. A bruised reed shall he not break, and the smoking flax shall he not quench: he shall bring forth judgment unto truth.
>
> **Isaiah 42:2-3**

> And he said unto me, My grace is sufficient for thee: for my strength is made perfect in weakness. Most gladly therefore will I rather glory in my infirmities, that the power of Christ may rest upon me.
>
> **2 Corinthians 12:9**

Calamus denotes the ability to endure those difficult, hard-to-handle events that face us in life. There are some challenges you're going to have to "wade through" in your walk with God. This is a brokenness that has noticeable effects. Calamus at work in one's life produces an odor that amplifies everything negative. It is good to know that even with issues and human weaknesses, God makes us sufficiently strong to handle every challenge that comes our way. He doesn't add more afflictions onto those who are genuinely broken before Him in this way; and He gives us strength to endure.

Cassia

The final ingredient was cassia, which is very similar to cinnamon. It is also harvested from the outer bark of a plant grown in India. [7]The fragrant part could not be obtained without a peeling process. This denotes those times when the Holy Spirit has to peel or strip away things that hinder the flow of the Spirit. He does this through the trials that come into our life.

> It is good for me that I have been afflicted; that I might learn Thy statues.
>
> **Psalm 119:71**

The name cassia comes from the Hebrew word *qiddâh*, meaning to shrivel up in a roll, and is linked to the thought of bowing (bending the head, body, or neck in deference).[8] In this way, it represents humility.

This speaks to us of Jesus Christ, who traded in His kingly garments and took on the form of a servant. Why? He loved humanity so much that He willingly "humbled Himself." When understood in the proper context, this should change the way we relate to others. What cassia represents is actually the opposite of selfish ambition or vainglory.

> Let this mind be in you, which was also in Christ Jesus: Who, being in the form of God, thought it not robbery to be equal with God: But made himself of no reputation, and took upon him the form of a servant, and was made in the likeness of men: And being found in fashion as a man, he humbled himself, and became obedient unto death, even the death of the cross. Wherefore God also hath highly exalted him…
>
> **PHILIPPIANS 2:5-9**

Believers must humble self in order to worship God, and while it may be unpleasant in the present, it will lead to being lifted up in God's due timing (Jas. 4:10). When cassia is at work, one can go the distance for the purpose of affecting change and glorifying Jesus Christ.

Spiritual maturity is sticking with the process in spite of the difficulties involved.

We receive the anointing, not to serve ourselves, but to affect the world around us for the glory of God. Putting these ingredients together gives us a picture of one who has been "smeared" with the oil of God. It is characterized by the graces of the Spirit released under pressure (olive oil); the bitter truth (myrrh); sweetness in the midst of trial and confidence in God's unfailing love (cinnamon); God's strength in the midst of weakness (calamus); and the humility of a servant's heart (cassia).

> Yea, and all that will live godly in Christ Jesus shall suffer persecution.
>
> **2 Timothy 3:12**

> As many as desire to make a fair shew in the flesh, they constrain you to be circumcised; only lest they should suffer persecution for the cross of Christ.
>
> **Galatians 6:12**

There are many obstacles one faces on this pathway. There are battles with the world, the flesh, the devil. Suffering is a part of the experience, but it's how we come through the suffering that really shapes us. Even Jesus had to learn obedience by the things He suffered—how much more do we, when there is bark of the flesh that needs to be scraped and peeled from our lives so we can be more effective? Spiritual maturity sticks with the process so they can "become" what they were called to "be."

> If ye endure chastening, God dealeth with you as with sons; for what son is he whom the father chasteneth not? …Now no chastening for the present seemeth to be

joyous, but grievous: nevertheless afterward it yieldeth the peaceable fruit of righteousness unto them which are exercised thereby. Wherefore lift up the hands which hang down, and the feeble knees; And make straight paths for your feet, lest that which is lame be turned out of the way; but let it rather be healed.

Hebrews 12:6-13

God wants us to be holy, so He disciplines us so we can share in His holiness. Sonship is a position of honor and privilege, but it comes with responsibility as well. Being a son or a daughter is in contrast to being a servant. So the correction comes for our benefit. God disciplines us out of His love. There are right and wrong ways to respond to His loving correction, including: giving up, taking it too lightly, or allowing it to cripple us by thinking He is being too harsh. Sonship means submitting oneself to fatherly discipline, and this is linked to separating from whatever is not pleasing to Him (2 Cor. 6:17-18).

Submission to spiritual authority is important. Someone needs to oversee the progress of your anointing and your spiritual growth and development. Sons and daughters who serve will take the time to sit under anointed leadership and bear the necessary fruit that qualifies them to move forward. One may be anointed, and yet it must be tested, verified, authenticated, if you will.

For though ye have ten thousand instructors in Christ, yet have ye not many fathers: for in Christ Jesus I have begotten you through the gospel.

1 Corinthians 4:15

Flowing Together

What does it mean to have wheat, oil, and wine flowing together in our lives? It means God has a purpose for His church! God gathers His redeemed people to show His manifold wisdom. Paul explains to the Ephesians that he was entrusted to declare the mystery of the church—and it was only through God's effective power (anointing) that he was able to do it. He felt humbled and honored that God would grace him this way.

> Unto me, who am less than the least of all saints, is this grace given, that I should preach among the Gentiles the unsearchable riches of Christ; And to make all men see what is the fellowship of the mystery, which from the beginning of the world hath been hid in God, who created all things by Jesus Christ: To the intent that now unto the principalities and powers in heavenly places might be known by the church the manifold wisdom of God.

Ephesians 3:8-10

We must affect this generation NOW. This means laying aside all of the things that the anointing is NOT, and experiencing the fullness of what it truly is. The altar, the incense, and the oil give us valuable principles to help us see how God continues to bring us through every challenge we may face, even when we aren't aware He is helping us. Everything God uses endures a process of crushing, breaking, peeling, grinding, and being compounded into something that honors Jesus Christ with its sweet fragrance that permeates every atmosphere where the anointing is in operation.

The End

Study Guide

This study guide may be used by individuals or small groups. Questions marked "Discuss" are more suitable to group discussion, while questions marked "Journal" are for one's personal reflection and growth. Readers are encouraged to keep a personal journal to record their responses. At the beginning of each review section there is a recap from the associated chapter.

Chapter 1

The Altar & The Incense

RECAP:

The articles of worship in the Tabernacle are all types and symbols related to the Person and work of Christ, and to our position in relationship with Him. The Altar of Incense, a type of Christ our intercessor, is unique in its construction and significant in its placement.

The priests burned incense twice a day—morning and evening. This coincided with sacrifices, the trimming of the lamps, and the setting out of fresh bread. The incense in the sanctuary acted as a fumigant, offsetting the smell coming from the brazen altar in the Outer Court. This meant that the scent lingered all day and night.

1. **Discuss**: The Mosaic Tabernacle contained two altars—a brazen altar for the sacrifices, and a Golden Altar in the Holy Place on which the holy incense was to be burned. What does this imagery tell you about the place of prayer and worship in the plan of God?

2. **Journal**: What is your prayer life like? What have been some of your most profound moments in worship? How important is it to you to know that Jesus Christ lives to make intercession for

His people?

3. **Discuss**: We talk a lot about Christ being at the center of it all. What does that mean in this world of constant busyness and communication, events and activity?

4. **Discuss**: If God knows what He will do anyway, why should we pray? How are our prayers incorporated into the eternal purpose of God for the world, or in our individual lives?

Chapter 2

Prayer & Intercession

RECAP:

Spirit-filled believers are called to cover each other in prayer. Corporate prayer has its own dynamic. Sometimes you've got to find an agreer to get the breakthrough. God's presence is there, wherever two or three are gathered in His name (Matt. 18:19-20). Pray until something happens!

The altar of prayer is the place for expression of relationship, requests, and claiming God's promises. But sin and impure motives can hinder prayer. It's not just how one asks, but what one asks for and why one asks for it, that matters. The Spirit leads to repentance through conviction (not condemnation!), so you can ask and receive with fullness of joy.

1. **Discuss**: Study the words *anointed* and *consecrated*. Why do you think they are connected? What do these words tell you about the character of God and the nature of anointed ministry?

2. **Discuss**: What does it mean to follow the leading or flow of the Holy Spirit?

3. **Journal**: Do you meditate often on who God is (His holy character, attributes, and identity) or more on what He does (His ways, actions)? Why do you think this is so?

4. **Project**: Read 1 Tim. 2:15 and Eph. 6:18-19. If you don't already have one, create a prayer list that includes these various groups of people. Commit to following it for one (1) week, then record the results.

5. **Journal**: Have you ever invested yourself in the ministry of intercession, or felt an urgent need to pray for someone else? Write about the experience.

6. **Discuss**: What is sanctification? When or how does it take place? Give at least three (3) scriptures to support your answer.

Scripture Meditation: John 14:16-17

For Further Study: The book of Acts

Chapter 3

From Blessing to Presence

RECAP:

The Holy Spirit gives us a new nature capable of displaying Christ's character (Eph. 4:24). This produces real change in a person's life—making him or her a "partaker of the divine nature" (2 Pet. 1:4). In other words, the Holy Spirit produces a holy people.

The anointing is our source of spiritual life and effectiveness. In fact, we are commanded to be filled with the Spirit (Eph. 5:18). But the anointing comes from God alone, and is not man-made. It has a "formula," and "ingredients" as we learn through the incense and the anointing oil, that can't be duplicated, bought, sold, controlled, or concocted artificially. It is real, genuine, and authentic.

1. **Discuss**: What is holiness? What are some of the first things that come to mind when you hear this word?

2. **Discuss**: Why are we required to give an account to God and others about the breath of life or the anointing? **Journal**: Do you have safe relationships in your life in which you can be accountable to others? Why or why not?

3. **Discuss**: What are the differences between petition, supplication, intercession, and travail? **Journal**: What is your prayer life like? How much time do you invest in making requests for others?

4. **Discuss**: Why do you think God set boundaries, warnings, and prohibitions around His presence? **Journal**: When have you experienced "putting off" something in order to draw nearer to God? What kind of impact did it have on your life?

Scripture Meditation: Rom 12:1-2; 1 Pet. 2:15-16

Chapter 4

Kingdom Connectors

RECAP:

The Word, Worship and Warfare connect us to the beauty and majesty of Jesus Christ! …God wants us to know Him and be filled with His fullness. This signifies the capacity to understand and execute His will in every area of life. In short, it is a partnership that becomes our standard and way of life.

God establishes Himself in our lives through His Word. We must follow carefully where God leads and manage our internal conflicts through submission to His rule and lordship. Know when God is moving and always move at His pace. This will demonstrate your life's defining moments. It will serve as proof that you are in His perfect will and understand the capacity and capability of your God.

1. **Discuss**: What are some of the ways you celebrate your relationship with God? **Journal:** How can deliberate acts of worship become more a part of how you relate to God daily, if they aren't already?

2. **Discuss**: Review the armor of God in Ephesians 6:10-18, and what each piece means. How do you suit up in this armor daily?

Journal: Write about a time when getting into God's presence led to a different perspective on a troubling situation. Did the problem ever change, or did God change your vantage point and give you new grace to endure it?

3. **Discuss:** What does it mean to be "in the Spirit?" What are some of the roles that the Holy Spirit plays in our lives daily? What happens when one of these "kingdom connectors" is lacking in our life?

Scripture Meditation: Col. 3:16-17; 2 Tim. 1:7

Chapter 5
The Wheat

RECAP:

The Word renews our minds and transforms our thinking (Rom. 12:2). Sadly, some are unwilling to change their ideas or opinions, and remain stuck. Change comes to the teachable spirit who does not mind being confronted with truth. But it's not just the word we "know," but what's hidden in our heart that keeps guards against sin (Ps. 119:11).

The "digestion" of spiritual truth denotes prevention against the discouragements, doubts, and distractions that come our way in life. When we speak of our revelation of Him through the Word, we touch the reality of who God is to us. Just as the prophets of old knew God as Jehovah-Jireh or Jehovah-Nissi, when we touch Him, we now move beyond mere human comprehension, we touch God Himself.

1. **Discuss**: What does wheat represent? How does the process of turning raw wheat into bread reflect the spiritual processes at work in our lives?

2. **Discuss**: Review the Parable of the Sower in Matthew 13. What

does it mean to have a heart that is good ground for the seed of the Word?

3. **Discuss**: An active life in the Word of God involves devotional reading, meditation on truth, and study. What is the difference between them? **Journal**: How much time do you spend reading the Bible? Do you understand what you read? If not, what practical steps can you take to learn more?

4. **Journal**: How do you hear the Word of God? Do you prayerfully consider what it is saying, in order to put it into practice? When has taking some aspect of God's truth to heart resulted in an increased capacity to receive from Him in your life?

5. **Journal**: Is the Word of God a priority in your life, or is it just something you listen to or read "when you have time?" How can this be maintained if it's already prioritized, or how can this be corrected if it isn't? What practical steps can you take?

6. **Discuss**: The kingdom of heaven is described as being a mixture of good and evil. What does this mean? How does Jesus say He will deal with the wheat? How does He say He will deal with the chaff? Give scriptures to support your answer.

Scripture Meditation: John 8:32; 1 Pet. 1:23

Chapter 6

The Wine

RECAP:

The real purpose of the Law—which is to reveal sin. It shows the strict justice of God and proves that all are sinners by nature and practice (Rom. 3:20-23). But the gospel gives us everything: cleansing through the blood, a new spiritual nature, and the power to live a holy life (Rom. 3:24-26). Spiritually, we are called to connect with God, investing ourselves in good works that bring glory to Him.

As you allow Him to bring the pruning and purging work of correction into your life, fruit, more fruit, and much fruit will come in its successive seasons. Then you will reach a place of maturity in God that understands the process and is fully submitted to its phases and experiences.

1. **Discuss**: God promises that He is a rewarder of those who diligently seek Him. How does one go about doing that? What is the difference between believing in God and believing God?

2. **Journal**: Write about your first or last occasion taking communion? If you have not participated recently, ask yourself

why. What does the blood of Jesus mean to you personally?

3. **Discuss**: Clearly, believers are to be those whose lives produce fruit for God. What exactly *is* that fruit? Give at least two (2) scriptures to support your answer.

4. **Journal**: When have you experienced the pruning hand of God in your life? How did you endure the process as you were going through it? What did you learn about God at the end of that experience?

Scripture Meditation: John 15:1-27

Chapter 7
The Oil

RECAP:

The anointing oil was comprised of five ingredients. Pure olive oil was the base, and myrrh, cinnamon, cassia, and calamus were added to it. Just as the incense, each ingredient had to be gathered and prepared separately before it could reach a usable state. Each element will give us some insight into the nature of the true anointing.

"The good news is that God does not discard the sap that has been cut out of our lives; God has a purpose for everything that we have gone through or will be going through. He allows us to identify the "bitter" in someone else who may be a babe in Christ—and it is our responsibility to guide and restore that person to the truth. We can do this because we have both the bitter truth and a balance of the anointed oils working in us" (Thomas 2012).

1. **Journal**: Have you ever pursued an understanding of biblical hermeneutics or typology? Why or why not? What steps might you take to familiarize yourself with this aspect of biblical teaching?

2. **Discuss**: What are the main ingredients used in the anointing

oil and what does each one represent spiritually?

3. **Journal**: Can you see any or all of these ingredients at work in your life? What is your response to adversity and suffering? How do you respond to the chastening of the Father in your life?

4. **Discuss**: What do you think of when you hear the words "process" or "submission?" What about the word "ministry?" **Journal**: What can you learn from the way Jesus endured His sufferings and emerged victoriously that can help you in the present moment?

5. **Journal:** Write about a recent "myrrh season" in your life. How did it expose you to some aspect of the truth? Did you emerge from the situation better than you were before? Why or why not?

6. **Discuss**: Why is it a mistake to confuse giftedness alone with the anointing of the Spirit? What biblical safeguards are in place to keep us from falling into this trap? Give scriptures to support your answer.

Scripture Meditation: Rom. 5:3-5; Heb. 5:7-9

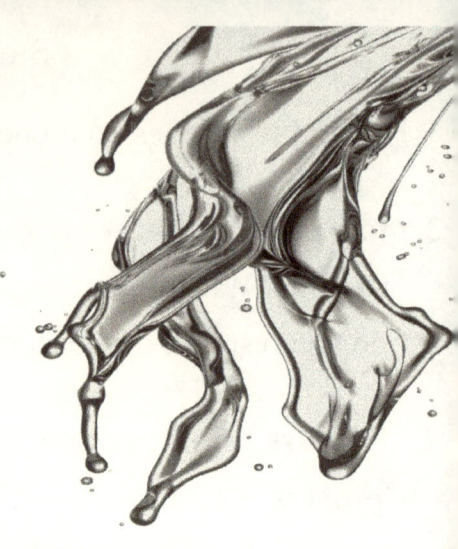

NOTES

CHAPTER 1

1. *Matthew Henry's Concise Commentary,* "Ex. 30:1-10" (1708-14, public domain), e-sword v. 10.3.0.

2. *John Wesley's Explanatory Notes,* "Ex. 30:10" (1755-66), e-sword v. 10.3.0.

3. *John Gill's Exposition of the Entire Bible,* "Ex. 30:3" (1748-63, 1809, public domain), e-sword v. 10.3.0.

4. Keil, Carl Friedrich and Franz Delitzsch, *Keil & Delitzsch Commentary on the Old Testament,* "Ex. 30:34-38" (1866-91, public domain), e-sword v. 10.3.0.

5. *Adam Clarke's Commentary on the Bible,* "Ex. 30:34" (1810-26, public domain), e-sword v. 10.3.0.

6. Ibid. Also Gill, "Ex. 30:34."

7. Strong, James, S.T.D., LL.D, *Strong's Bible Dictionary*, "H7826," and "H7827," (1890).

8. Keil and Delitzsch, "Ex. 30:34-38."

9. Exell, Joseph S. (ed.), *The Biblical Illustrator*, "Matt. 2:11," (1905-09, public domain), e-sword v. 10.3.0.

CHAPTER 2

1. *Strong's Bible Dictionary*, "G4436."

2. *John Gill's Exposition of the Entire Bible*, "Lev. 10:2" (1748-1809).

3. Ibid., "Lev. 10:2"

4. MacLaren, Alexander, *Expositions of Holy Scripture*, "Lev. 10:1-11," (1904-1910, public domain), e-sword v. 10.3.0.

5. See Note 2. 2 Cor. 2:15

CHAPTER 3

1. *Strong's Bible Dictionary*, "G42."

2. Ibid. "G5548"

3. Thayer, Joseph H., *Thayer's Greek Definitions*, "G37," (1886-1889, public domain), e-sword v. 10.3.0.

4. See Note 1. Header words are as follows: yitshâr, H3323; shemen, H808 and mimshach, H4473.

5. Ibid. Header words are as follows: epichriō, G2025 and mimshach, G346. For chriō, see Note 2.

CHAPTER 4

1. Forsyth, Peter, *Positive Preaching and Modern Mind*, p. 200, AC Armstrong & Son, New York (1907). https://archive.org/stream/positivepreachin00fo siala#page/200/mode/2up. Accessed September 11, 2015.

2. Scofield, C.I., *Scofield's Reference Notes* (1917). See 1 Pet. 2:9 for full explanation.

3. *Adam Clarke's Commentary on the Bible*, "John 4:24."

4. *Thayer's Greek Definitions*, "G3794."

5. For an exhaustive discussion of professionalism versus the anointing, see *The Making of a Leader* by Frank Damazio.

CHAPTER 5

1. *Albert Barnes' Notes on the Bible*, "Luke 6:1."

2. Ibid., "Lev. 26:3-45" and "Deut. 11:14."

3. Ibid., "Jer. 4:3."

4. *Adam Clarke's Commentary on the Bible*, "Isa. 25:10" and "Jer. 51:2."

5. *Albert Barnes' Notes on the Bible*, "Psa. 139:3" and "Isa. 41:16."

6. Keil &Delitzsch, "Judges 6:11-32."

7. *John Gill's Exposition of the Entire Bible*, "Matt. 13:20."

8. Schaff, Philip ed. *Popular Commentary*, "Matthew 13:23," (1879-90, public domain), e-sword v. 10.3.0.

CHAPTER 6

1. Smith, William, *Smith's Bible Dictionary*, "Wine" (1901). Also Faussett, A.R., *Fausset's Bible Dictionary*, "Wine" (1888).

2. Ibid.

3. *Albert Barnes' Notes on the Bible*, "Isa. 33:9."

4. Ibid., "Isa. 65:10."

5. *Matthew Henry's Concise Commentary*, "Matt. 26:26-30."

6. Watts, Isaac and Ralph E. Hudson, "Alas, and Did My Savior Bleed?" (1707-1885), http://cyberhymnal.org/htm/a/l/a/alasand.htm, accessed Oct. 28, 2015

CHAPTER 7

1. *Smith's Bible Dictionary*, "Olive."

2. *Adam Clarke's Commentary on the Bible*, "Ex. 27:20."

3. *John Gill's Exposition of the Entire Bible*, "Ex. 30:23."

4. *Strong's Bible Dictionary*, "H7076."

5. *Albert Barnes' Notes on the Bible*, "Matt. 11:7."

6. Ibid., "Isa. 42:3."

7. Ibid., "Ex. 30:22-33."

BIBLIOGRAPHY

Barnes, Albert. "Albert Barnes' Notes on the Bible." (1847-85).

Clarke, Adam. "Adam Clarke's Commentary on the Bible." (1810-26).

Connor, Kevin. "The Tabernacle of Moses." Portland: City Bible Publishing, 1976.

Damazio, Frank. "The Making of a Leader." Portland: City Bible Publishing, 1988.

Exell, Joseph S. (ed.), "The Biblical Illustrator." (1905-09).

Faussett, A.R., "Fausset's Bible Dictionary." (1888).

Forsyth, Peter. "Positive Preaching and Modern Mind." New York: AC Armstrong & Son, 1907. https://archive.org/stream/positivepreachin00forsiala#page/200/mode/2up.

Gill, John. "John Gill's Exposition of the Entire Bible." (1748-63, 1809).

Halderman, I.M. "The Tabernacle Priesthood and Offerings." Revell Fleming Company, 1925.

Hagee, John. "His Glory Revealed: A Prophetic Devotional." Nashville: Thomas Nelson, 1999.

Hanby, Mark. "Anointing the Unsanctified." Shippensburg: Destiny Image Publishers, 1993.

Hanby, Mark. "Perceiving the Wheel of God." Shippensburg: Destiny Image Publishers, PA, 1994.

Henry, Matthew. "Matthew Henry's Concise Commentary" (1708-1714).

Keil, Carl Friedrich and Franz Delitzsch. "Keil & Delitzsch Commentary on the Old Testament." (1866-91).

MacLaren, Alexander. "Expositions of Holy Scripture." (1904-1910).

Ryken, Leland, James C. Wilhoit, Tremper Longman III, eds. "Dictionary of Biblical Imagery." Downers Grove: InterVarsity Press USA, 1998.

Schaff, Philip, ed. "Popular Commentary." (1879-90).

Scofield, C.I., "Scofield's Reference Notes." (1917).

Stern, David H. "Jewish New Testament Commentary." Clarksville: Jewish New Testament Publications, Inc., 1992.

Strong, James, S.T.D., LL.D, "Strong's Bible Dictionary." (1890).

Thayer, Joseph H., "Thayer's Greek Definitions." (1886-1889).

Thomas, Walter and Jean A. Elster, ed. "Spiritual Navigation for the 21st Century." Judson PR, 2000.

Watts, Isaac and Ralph E. Hudson, "Alas, and Did My Savior Bleed?" (1707-1885), http://cyberhymnal.org/htm/a/l/a/alasand.htm.

Wesley, John. "John Wesley's Explanatory Notes." (1755-66).

www.ingramcontent.com/pod-product-compliance
Lightning Source LLC
LaVergne TN
LVHW041626070426
835507LV00008B/480